Martial Arts: Behi
The Martial Arts and Self Defense S(

"A must read for all martial arts practitioners and enthusiasts"

"Well-written and entertaining."

"A fun, enjoyable and quirky read"

Phil Pierce

Copyright © 2015

For Your Free Book visit:
www.BlackBeltFit.com

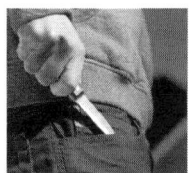   

What Can You Get From This Book?

- Do you know the best martial art for 'real' street self-defense?

- Or how board breaking really works – and how you can do it?

- Uncover the one self-defense myth that will keep you alive!

- The truth behind martial arts superhumans

- Which is the original martial art?

- The truth about your inner badass

- The surprising reality behind everyone's favourite weapon

- What meditation can really do for you

- The secret 'trick' to Bruce Lee's One Inch Punch

- And more!

The simple aim of this short book is to unlock some of the mysteries and legends surrounding Martial Arts and give you an informative (and sometimes humorous) insight into this esoteric world!

Whether you are just thinking about starting out or have been training for years the tips and topics in this guide can help you better understand the crazy world of Martial Arts and some of the myths surrounding it.

Ever wondered if some of the abilities you see in the movies are achievable? Or what will really keep you safe on the street?

You may be surprised at the answers...

Your Free Bonus Book (and Audiobook)!

Do you want to learn how to develop explosive power for Martial Arts, Fitness and more?

Grab your Completely Free bonus book (or Audiobook); **"3 Steps to Explosive Power"** now!

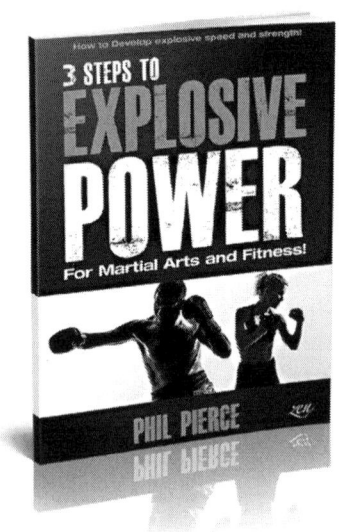

Just head over to my site:

www.BlackBeltFit.com

Claim your copy now!

Contents

What Can You Get From This Book?	2
From the Author	7
Your Inner Badass	11
A note on Adrenaline:	15
The Truth about Knives in Self Defense	17
How to Test Your Skills against a 'Knife'	22
Which is the Most Effective Martial Art for Self-Defense?	24
Self Defense Recommendations:	28
The Ancient Secret of…	30
Traditional Styles vs. Modern	39
The "Best" Martial Art of All	44
How to Choose the 'Best' Martial Art for YOU	50
Pressure Points and the Touch of Death	53
Pressure Points You Can Use	61
Martial Arts Superpowers	64
Almost Everything You Know About Ninjas	72
The Legendary Samurai Sword	79
Bulletproof Monks and Martial Toughness	85
How You Can 'Toughen Up'	93
The Secret to Breaking Boards	96
How can I do it?	101
Meditation and Martial Arts Magic	105

Using Relaxation for Attack and Defence	111
Which is the 'Original' Martial Art?	118
A Timeline of Martial Arts	124
Bruce Lee; the Legend, the Myths…	128
The One-Inch Punch (and How you can do it)	132
Thank you (and a Free Book!)	139
Ready for More?	142

From the Author

Firstly let me start by saying that I love Martial Arts and I owe them a great debt.

Many years ago I was jumped one evening while walking past a local bar. The unprovoked attack left me requiring surgery and many hospital visits. The incident also had significant psychological ramifications.

Instead of accepting the unfortunate event and moving on I spent a long time turning my frustration inwards. For months I blamed myself for that night and this lead to a period of depression that I now see as probably the low point of my life. Oh sure, the actual punk that mugged me did the physical damage (and was never caught by the way) but like most 18 year old guys I had always thought that in a tight spot I could handle myself and turn on the "tough guy" as required.

It was only after I'd spent 30 seconds choking on my own blood wondering if I was about to die in that silly little town that I realized all the bravado, all the posturing and fooling around with my friends counted for exactly nothing. There was no "Tough Guy" to switch on.

This absolute demolition of my ego triggered a long period of depression, in which my grades bombed, my family and friends became alienated and I rarely left the house.

I could write at length about that time but that's not what this book is about. Suffice to say I was in a bad place.

Eventually a friend suggested I accompany him to a local 'demonstration' in an effort to get me back out in the world. I agreed to attend but his cryptic description left me wondering the nature of the event.

Global Warming? Animal Welfare? Protestors against Reality Television? I wondered what this 'demonstration' would be all about.

Martial Arts as it turned out. Specifically a nearby TaeKwonDo school opening its doors to recruit new students.

I was sceptical for certain, but right from the start of the action I was impressed. Here were a bunch of people who, regardless of the art in question, were extremely fit, very positive and damned skilful. I became enraptured during that hour and signed up the next day.

As the weeks went by the fine medical staff of the local hospital took care of the bruises and scars on the outside, while the local Taekwondo School took care of my sanity on the inside.

Initially Tae Kwon Do was nothing more than a couple hours' break from moping around the house. However, I soon found that I loved the structured learning and that my fitness was fast increasing fast.

As the years went by I not only physically recovered but also far surpassed my former narrow minded approach to life; developing a greater understanding of body and mind. My horizons broadened as I became fascinated with the fitness, ethics and techniques of Taekwondo and upon reaching Black belt I started delving into understanding other Martial Arts, attending seminars and classes learning elements of Self Defence, Personal Awareness and coaching. My search even took me to the Far East where I have spent months in China, Japan and Thailand learning at the source.

I've loved every minute of it.

The aim of this book is not to poke fun at any styles. Rather, it is meant to expose the popular, fallacious and potentially dangerous stereotypes that have sprung up surrounding them, based on my experiences. And then perhaps poke fun at these.

This guide has been created to explain many things I wish I had known when starting out in the crazy world of Martial Arts and Self Defense, and help steer you in the right direction if you are new to it all, or if you are just looking to broaden your understanding of this often esoteric world.

Some of the topics within this book include hard facts, while others include philosophical concepts and some of my own musings. All with the aim of giving you the chance to make an informed decision of your own.

So let it be said again, I love Martial Arts – all of them. They all have beneficial aspects and bring so much happiness to the people that practice them. X art is not better than Y art, (they are just different) and no style is without value. Except Capoeira you big bunch of dancing girls. (Just kidding)

Today I'm lucky enough to have achieved Black belt and Instructor level in several styles and I've managed to train with some of the best Martial Artists around the world. It's also interesting (some might say ironic) that I've never had any trouble on the streets since that night.

People still sometimes say to me "If you ever saw that guy that mugged you again what would you do?"

I usually reply "I never saw him the first time!"

I hope you find this book entertaining, useful and eye-opening.

- *Phil*

Your Inner Badass

In a tight spot could you switch on your inner tough-guy?

I wanted to open by addressing the most difficult myth for most of us to admit to.

So you've done a few years of Martial Arts. Or perhaps you've not done any official training but you are in reasonable shape or you are a big guy. You could probably pull it out of the bag if you were ever threatened in a real violent encounter right?

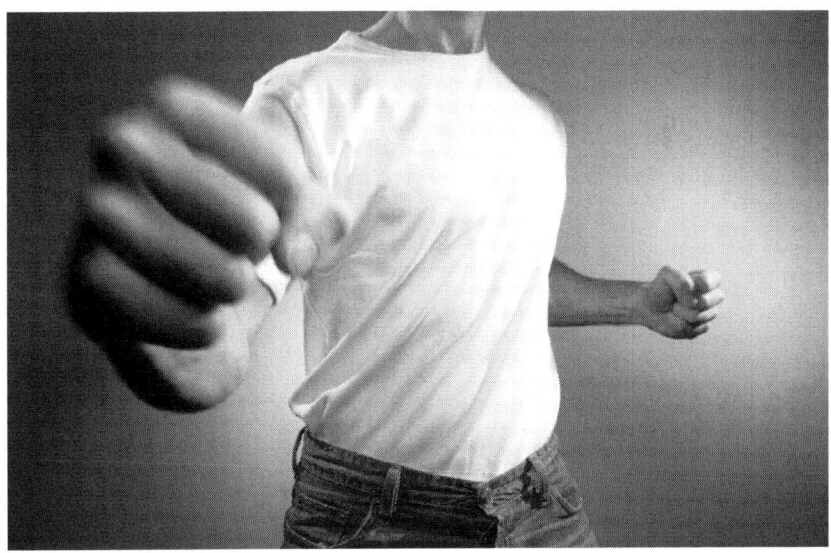

Actually, you probably couldn't. It was in fact this realization that I found hardest to deal with after I was assaulted. But as the years have gone by I have discovered it's not arrogance or teenage macho posturing that made me badly misjudge my abilities. The truth is we ALL do it…ALL the time…no matter what age we may be.

This reality is one of the hardest to accept and even reading now it's likely you are already thinking *"oh this doesn't apply to me"* or *"I'm different"* but be aware that psychological studies have demonstrated the tendency is almost universal. In fact thinking you are different is demonstrating the process in action from the start.

It's down to a little case of something known as **'Illusory superiority'**. This is a proven condition we all suffer with regarding our daily aptitude in all things, not just fighting or self-defense.

For example in a given group 80% of individuals might typically think they can run a 400m track faster than average. But when tested only 20% of them really can.

It's sometimes also called the **'Above Average Effect'** and essentially it means that for much of your life you will personally value yourself slightly better at things than those around you. It's this same effect that also makes you think you could probably take on anyone in a fight or god forbid, a life-threatening situation and win.

This cognitive bias, first officially named in 1991 has now become a staple of modern psychology and has been tested across intelligence assessments, physical performance and even social interaction.

It's also closely tied to a similar condition called the Dunning-Kruger effect, partly named after David Dunning, renowned researcher on the subject. He claims Illusory Superiority is more common than you might think and goes on to call it the "the anosognosia of everyday life". Or put simply a lack of subjective self-awareness in your daily existence.

There are numerous suggestions on the physical mechanisms behind why we do this but many theories suspect it is down to the manner in which our brains process complicated information into simpler, easier to manage estimates, usually in our own favor.

On the plus side it aids in motivation, giving us incentive to push forward in the knowledge we are doing well at something and it gives us confidence that we will succeed.

However, the downside is that we think we are proficient at things without any evidence to support the idea.

What this means from a Martial Artist's standpoint is that you probably aren't as good as you think. Bad news for training in class…even worse news on the street!

So what can I do?

Luckily knowing this is half of the battle. Now you are aware of the naturally biased brain we all carry around you can train appropriately. Yes you'll want to push yourself harder but you can also be aware that your own perspective is not to be trusted 100%. This makes you a more rounded and well-adjusted person, aware of your own limitations and abilities. Similarly you will know your opponent probably feels this somewhat mistaken superiority also. Whether you use this to your advantage is up to you.

Any decent self-defense or Martial Arts system practices with the assumption that your opponent is bigger, stronger and better trained than you are. If you embrace this ethos you can push yourself to become the Martial Artist you already think you are!

A note on Adrenaline:

Adrenaline is discussed in more detail within my best-selling self-defense book "How to Defend Yourself in 3 Seconds". Occasionally, alcohol or other narcotics can play an important role in violent encounters but Adrenaline is almost guaranteed to play a bigger one.

For most of us our daily lives contain very little conflict and minimal exposure to real aggression. When we are faced with a sudden unexpected and violent situation, the huge dump of adrenaline into your body will instantly cloud your judgment and mess with your senses.

It's because of this that much of what we would call 'technique' goes out of the window when life gets real and we resort to the primal fight or flight instinct. The inner badass suddenly becomes a confused and panicked brawler, flinging limbs around with wild abandon.

Be aware of this and also be aware that no matter how tough you think you are adrenaline can ruin even the best training when the pressure is on.

The Truth about Knives in Self Defense

Do blades work as a self-defense weapon?

Many of the topics in this book are fairly light-hearted observations based on the strange and occasionally silly world of Martial Arts but this is one myth that is not only dangerously incorrect but one that could also get you killed.

Blades are commonly, and perhaps erroneously, linked with Martial Arts due to their appearance in the media, wherein the lead uses some fancy techniques to incapacitate the antagonist.

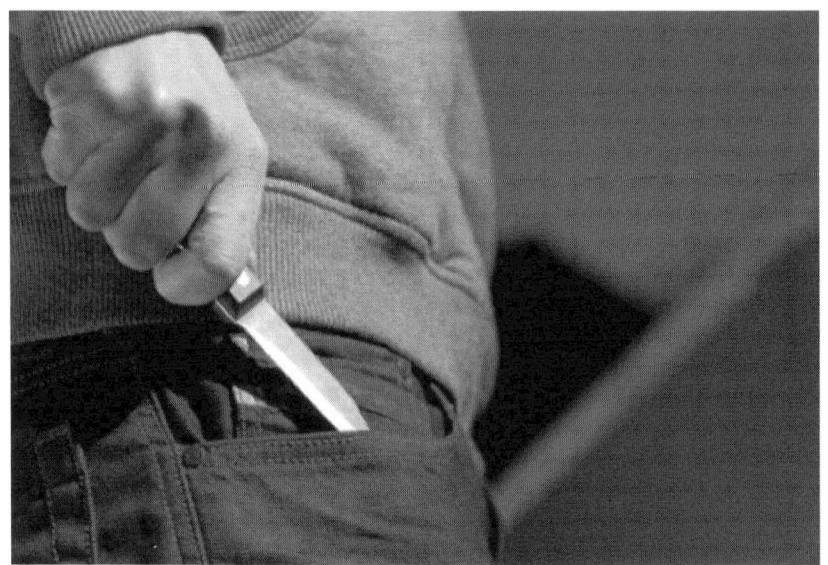

You may have seen in the movies where the hero (Possibly Steven Seagal) gets locked into a knife fight with his/her nemesis, the blades are flashing and the techniques are slick and smooth. (Just like Seagal's hair)

The reality, however, is different on a deadly scale.

Knives are messy, awkward and ultimately very dangerous for all involved, not just the defender, and edged weapons are more closely tied to pure self-defense than Martial Arts.

If you are thinking about choosing to carry a blade for self-protection the question you really have to ask yourself is what type of blade would you like to get stabbed by? Because this is the reality of knife violence.

Admittedly much of the modern world is civilized enough to realize that carrying a deadly weapon is not a great idea in any circumstance, but among gang culture and the realm of one-upmanship perpetrated on the streets, many people still believe what they see on the movies; that knives are easy to use and there is always a clear winner and loser.

Some people erroneously believe knives:

- May offer a status symbol
- May offer protection
- Are safe in a pocket
- Might give you control

The truth is much more of a fuzzy, blood stained line.

Not only is carrying a knife with the intention of use against another person illegal in most parts of the world but in a violent altercation you are massively more likely to get stabbed yourself if you carry a knife. Police statistics from around the world back this up with grisly reports of stabbing victims daily.

In the UK alone, government statistics report over 4000 people annually admitted into hospital as victims of assault via a sharp object. Interestingly the term 'victim' in this case only refers to being on the receiving end of the injury and receiving treatment by medical personnel – not to the person who carried the weapon originally.

One could argue that stabbings in other parts of the world are much higher, but one can't go by statistics alone because many injuries may go unreported.

If you are still in doubt ask any law enforcement officer, security officer or self-defense coach. The Metropolitan Police even go on record making it quite simple: *"By carrying a knife, you are much more likely to get stabbed yourself."*

The reason is two-fold.

1. By carrying a knife you have escalated a potentially violent situation to a potentially fatal one. Even if your opponent was only going to beat you up he now knows it's life or death – probably yours.

2. You have introduced a weapon to the arena. Fights are scrappy, not clean cut, and even a slight knock can jolt that knife from your hand or pocket. Guess what – you've just given your opponent a way to kill you!

Even if your enemy doesn't manage to grab your weapon and you are able to get a few swipes it's incredibly easy to drop (hello slashed legs) or stumble over and stab yourself.

Real self-defense training against knives generally advises to keep as much distance as possible and not getting involved at all if this can be achieved. Running away might feel cowardly or dishonorable but you'll still be alive to think it! Only after eliminating all alternatives should you engage a blade-wielding threat.

Famed Self-Defense Coach and Author Geoff Thompson goes on to say: *"If a knife is pulled and running away is not on the option list, throw anything that isn't nailed to the floor at the attacker, and then run"*

A popular Self-Defense adage sums it up nicely:

"The difference between the winner and loser in a knife fight? One dies at the scene, the other dies later in hospital"

How to Test Your Skills against a 'Knife'

If you'd like to see for yourself just how messy and difficult knife combat is grab a friend and try this fun exercise;

Note: ensure you both wear old T-Shirts!

- Grab a friend to work with and ensure you both wear light colored and old/inexpensive clothing

- Establish an area about 15ft square that you both must remain within

- Start by facing each other, a few feet away with hands up ready to move

- Set a watch or timer for 30 seconds

- One of you assumes the role of 'attacker' while the other becomes 'defender'

- The attacker uncaps the marker pen (try red for added effect!) and when the timer starts he/she is aiming to mark the 'defender' with a slashing motion on the body.

- The defender must move around and use only his/her hands to avoid getting marked in any way they see fit

- After 30 seconds, or if the pen is dropped, swap roles and try it again.

Naturally in a real-life scenario running away would be a preferable option but for this drill try 'defending yourself' against the pen. Give it just a few attempts and take a look at your clothing. You'll be shocked, I guarantee it.

Which is the Most Effective Martial Art for Self-Defense?

Which Martial Art is really the best for self-protection?

People take up Martial Arts for a variety of reasons; fitness, building confidence, camaraderie, because they saw 'The Karate Kid' and many more, but one of the most popular motivations is the desire to learn self-defense; to be able to look after yourself in a violent incident.

But herein lies one of the most widely propagated myths in the whole industry. Martial Arts are in fact **NOT** good for protecting yourself on the street.

At least not in the way most people think.

It may sound like I've just devalued the last 15 years of my life and anyone else that has years of Belts and Dojo time, but there is an important distinction in definition here.

Martial Arts in the traditional sense of the weekly Karate, TaeKwonDo or Kung Fu classes are completely different to dedicated Self-Defense classes but much confusion exists between the two. Unfortunately Martial Arts as a term has become synonymous for Self-Defense.

Now firstly understand that I'm not saying there is no value in the traditional styles. (Think White Gi, punching in rows etc.). These clubs help thousands of people achieve great things, like the aforementioned improvements in fitness, confidence and a sense of team spirit. As well as some often overlooked skills of distance, timing, leadership and focus.

The confusion lies in the way traditional arts are marketed as a method of modern self-defense when in fact they are distorted versions of techniques that may (or may not), have worked hundreds, if not thousands of years ago.

The danger here is that the average Shotokan black-belt might go into a mugging situation confident of his ability. Only to realise he isn't barefoot, his clothes are now restrictive and the surroundings aren't a nice clean gym as per usual.

Traditional 'big' Martial Arts like Karate, TaeKwonDo, Aikido, Kung Fu and many others have very limited real-world applications today. Even if the striking techniques are powerful they don't usually take into account the variables of adrenaline, multiple attackers and fighting from a disadvantaged position.

If you are purely in it to learn physical techniques to defend yourself then steer clear of the traditional styles.

*"There is nothing wrong with sport martial art, I love it, I am a big fan. And recreational training is better than no training at all. But if people are ever to survive a violent encounter on the pavement arena, it is imperative that they learn to distinguish between the two." – **Geoff Thompson, famed Author and Self Defense Coach***

Even the MMA'ers of the world, who often love to tell the traditional Martial Artists how much more effective their style is, find themselves bound by a number of rules in the arena (Where they are indeed very effective). Again though, there are none on the street.

There is a BIG difference between what I would call Martial Arts training and reality based Self-Defense training.

While classic Martial Artists learn in very rigid forms, modern systems, like Krav Maga, (Think Jason Bourne), what was known as Keysei, (Think Batman) or Systema (Think Russians) teach exposure to multiple attackers, weapons, adverse fighting conditions and brutally effective strikes and locks. The no-b.s approach to defending yourself.

For example one of the Shaolin sweeps I learned during my travels involved the practitioner dropping to the floor, placing the weight on the forward foot and spinning 360 degrees to bring his/her leg against the rear of an opponent's leg, hopefully toppling them, before climbing back to your feet.

The equivalent technique in modern styles is basically, step in, hook the opponent's front leg one way while pushing the chest the other. No going to the floor, no spinning and no time wasting. Twice as fast, just as effective.

Which do you think would be safer in a violent encounter?

If you are purely seeking to know how to physically dominate a mugging or attacker on the street these are the systems to look at.

But here's the thing, Martial Arts training, even in traditional styles, does prepare you in some hugely important areas that most people overlook, including; fitness, awareness, distance and timing.

The ability to be fit enough to escape a situation and smart enough to recognise a threat before it happens are arguably the two most valuable skills for 'real' self-defense. Way before any physical techniques are actually used. The 'old' styles also teach excellent principles of distance and timing – which becomes crucial if you are ever going to deliver effective strikes or blocks. Learning the physical sensation of how far and how quickly you can reach a target is the core of making any technique and this is something you practise over and over in arts when you hit pads, work in the dojo or spar with a partner.

For this reason the Karateka, Kung Fu students and Taekwondo players aren't quite down and out yet! These old-school styles still offer a fantastic foundation to build upon.

Ultimately don't believe that any 'one style' has all the answers. Try out a few yourself and find what works for you.

Self Defense Recommendations:

What many people call 'Traditional' Martial Arts offer great starting point in Self Protection even if they don't contain all the answers. Devote a few years to mastering one of these and you will develop a great basic understanding of your own body and its capabilities.

Once you achieve a good level in one of these I would then suggest specialising in another discipline depending on your needs. For pure self-defense 'modern' Arts offer no-nonsense tactical knowledge. For competition and all-round ability MMA is a fine direction to take or for more specific applications you can look to rarer styles.

The final tier is very specialised and involves pressure testing, full contact drills and high-impact training. This level may not be required for most people but for those looking for the ultimate self-defense challenge (and reward) you can look into one-on-one Military and Security training or taking your Modern Self-Defense style to Instructor level.

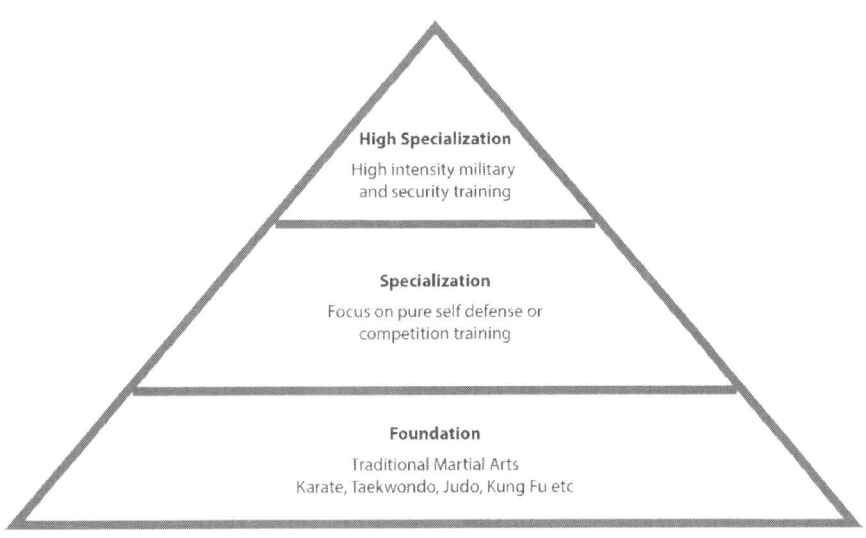

The Ancient Secret of...

Do Martial Arts hold secret knowledge even today?

Many people believe that after years of Martial Arts training and mental discipline there unlocks a gateway to ultra-secret knowledge reserved for only the most 'Zen' of masters, passed down from one generation to the next.

Perhaps you'd like to learn the meaning of life, the universe and everything from your Sensei. It's a popular concept after-all, especially within Movies and TV, that among the top tier and most wizened of martial-masters exists some ancient enlightenment only achieved through years of dedicated practice at a remote mountain top.

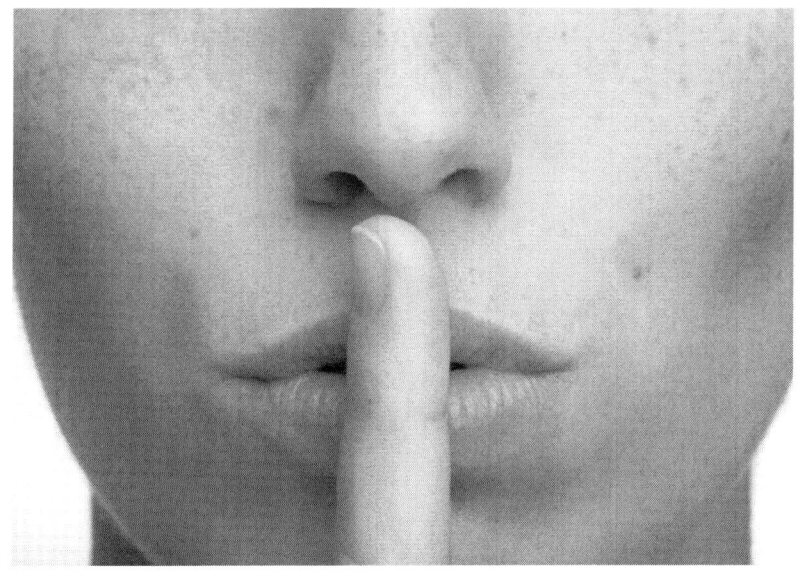

Ok, perhaps most people know that this is a bit of an exaggeration but even on a more realistic level many of us become involved in Martial Arts due to the lure of these secretive and legendary styles of combat and the knowledge they may unlock.

As students we often expect coaches to harbour some little nuggets of elite information that we will eventually receive when we are 'worthy' or have proven our aptitude after years of training. After all, we need something to aim for and the elusive concept of some esoteric reward is a tantalising prospect.

So what might this secret knowledge contain?

The ability to beat all others in combat? – We've already examined this idea in a future chapter. This kind of knowledge is not exactly secretive or rare.

Inner peace? – Meditation is greatly beneficial, but again no secret. See the later chapter.

Harmony of body and mind? - Perhaps. This concept is very personal but training can offer many benefits to both physical and mental ability.

Some unknown benefit? – The agnostic Martial Artist may think there are some hidden secrets that are impossible to comprehend until you reach the lofty heights of Black Belt or above. But then what are we aiming for while we learn?

The fact is that though some masters hold a stunning amount of wisdom, its source can usually be traced to more accessible and realistic means. Throughout life there is the opportunity to observe and learn from our mistakes and from those persons in our inner circle of peers. However this is not a supernatural body of information tapped into at will like a magic eight ball. Although the Eight Ball itself might make a good self-defence weapon...

More often than not, knowledge in Martial Arts is the result of a mixture of common sense, experience and lucky guesses.

This is not to say that Martial Arts operate free of knowledge. Indeed there is a vast collection of information that has been shared from one generation to the next. For example Wing Chun Kung Fu is often considered to be modelled on in-depth principles expressed in the classic Taote Ching – a deep and carefully thought out philosophical text and many styles of Shaolin training of course derive from knowledge of Buddhism and religious study. However these insights are just as accessible to scholars and researchers as they are to the Martial Artist.

Perhaps then we should look at the term itself. 'Martial' knowledge implies forms, techniques, strategies, methods of negotiating conflict, and ways of developing peace. However, there is nothing magic or secretive about it.

'Art' however, as we all know, is subjective. What one person considers beautiful or important is irrelevant to another. Could it then be argued that the search for insight is subjective since it is not called 'Martial Science'?

Chinese Whispers

The legend of Secret Knowledge in Martial Arts is the result of, ironically, Chinese Whispers. Information gets filtered through each individual's perceptions. As a child perhaps you played the game. Someone begins a whisper which travels from one participant's lips to another's ear. Eventually the last child gets to announce the message out loud. It is nearly always wrong, quite amusing and if played correctly can embarrass every parent within earshot.

What do you mean it started out Fuzzy Duck?!

Having tried the same game with adults I can tell you the inaccuracy is definitively not limited to young minds. In this same way Martial Arts and all the accompanying knowledge has been handed down, not through dozens of participants, but by thousands, millions even.

When combat styles were originally developing and being taught to others the training methods and philosophy of these early days would have been passed down orally – a method far more susceptible to different interpretations; which could account for many inaccuracies and hazy definitions of techniques even today. Multiply the potential for error over the generations and you will see that the chances of extremely precise and rare knowledge being accurately relayed from that era to this one rests near zero.

One could, of course, argue the fact that any such valuable knowledge wouldn't have been shared amongst the uneducated masses. In this case the secrets were only whispered to the dedicated few in the inner circle or top- tier. Before secrets were shared, they first passed a rigorous training regime that tested the spirit of both their body and mind.

Remember those awesome trials from films like Never Ending Story or Kill Bill? Well they were nothing like that. The tests were more likely simple affairs measuring endurance and strength of will. In modern terms think more a month without alcohol or a day with no internet.

Though the roots may be true, there is actually very little to suggest that the top tier of Martial Arts we see today strictly follows the intentions of the original founders at all.

There is an additional vulnerability in such a closed system. Since few can claim knowledge of a secret technique involved in each Martial Arts system, new followers can easily fall prey to those with less than honest intentions. Even those who mean well may unintentionally interject their own less than accurate thoughts as part of the learning, and who would there be to question the validity? Trained disciples are meant to trust their superiors with all their hearts and minds.

One final thought in this reasoning, is that the entire premise of a mystical body of knowledge suggests that such information is beyond our own capabilities today. If farmers and monks in the most primitive of times, without Lattes and IPhones, could render such intelligence, then why can't we as sophisticated, educated, and slightly caffeine addicted, individuals discover the same if not better information for ourselves, all without all the esoteric forms and austere sharing of secrets?

Each group or region would no doubt hold their own ideas of defence. However, this concept of a mystical knowledge somehow availing itself to high-level practitioners of one particular form or another seems a bit far-fetched.

This doesn't mean that Martial Arts are fake - that it is not worth your time, or fails to have a place in the modern world. There are amazing benefits to practicing one of the many marvellous systems out there. It just means that it isn't magic. There is no real 'secret' knowledge to tap into.

The Zen Approach

Regardless of what is written here many coaches will insist that a Black Belt is where it's at and you will finally 'understand' when you make the grade. A belt is just something that holds your pants up – as the old saying goes, but reaching Black Belt is an exciting prospect whoever you are.

Of course there are also the teachers who guide their students through seemingly wild goose chases and pointless exercises with the hope that eventually they will stumble upon their own insight.

But wait, is it pointless?

After all, practising a skill and learning to get better gives you completely unique insights into your own body and mind. Insights from a perspective no-one else could offer. 'Secrets' you might say.

In fact the 'Zen' philosophy from Buddhism – a source of inspiration for many Arts, teaches that mindful **experience** is the most valued path through life; more important than endless debate around what was or what might be. Zen is the focus of insight through the guided practise of understanding, usually with an accomplished mentor. That sounds pretty familiar to most Martial Arts students.

Could it then be said that the 'secret' to Martial Arts is actually found within the simple practise of them on a regular basis - ultimately what *you* discover from within?

It would make sense.

Traditional Styles vs. Modern

Do Older (Traditional) Styles Hold More Value?

Various forms of Martial Arts have been around for thousands of years. As long as there has been man, there has been conflict and as long as there has been conflict, people have needed methods of defense. Before guns and bombs there was a different type of combat. Men would defend their honor and land with little more than their bodies and a few strategically used primitive tools. The warriors during this time would easily also fit under the umbrella of 'Martial Arts'.

The organized Martial Arts, especially the Chinese styles that we are familiar with today, typically claim the Zhou Dynasty as their origin. More specifically, the yellow emperor, also known as Huangdi is attributed with the accomplishment of being the first to put such a system in writing somewhere between 1122 and 255 BC. His system, *Chang Quan*, or long fist, is considered the ancestor of many modern martial art forms. However, it would be naïve to assume that it was the very first system practiced. After all, humans have been fighting since they first figured out how to club each other with a stick.

Many lessons are passed down through the traditions of Martial Arts but we are not talking about the answers to the universe, merely simple and effective methods for attack and defense. It is with interest then that we see so many Martial Arts making increased claims of effectiveness based on age.

"Kung Fu is older than Shotokan Karate so it must be better"

"The new combat arts have no history or soul"

True enough the modern styles of combat lack the history of their predecessors, which may make them slightly less intriguing for enthusiasts or historians but what difference would this make to effectiveness?

Why should the most primitive of man eons ago possess greater knowledge than is available to us today? The mystique model simply does not add up.

With great age comes great…wisdom?

It is interesting to note that Martial Arts, is one of the few sects (another example being religion) to claim greater integrity based on its ancient roots. If you spend any time in the Martial Arts setting you might very well hear followers of various forms claim that their practice is more genuine because its foundation can be traced back an extra few hundred years. In a world that is new, modern, and at points uncertain, one can feel grounded and drawn into a practice with such timeless intrigue. But does age and mysticism really make a style more valid?

Let's think about it for a second. If you went to the doctor with a headache and he suggested Blood Letting or Electro-shock Therapy you'd probably think the poor MD had received a hardcopy of Gray's Anatomy to the head.

We now accept that the latest cutting edge research advances our knowledge of medicine every day and that primitive or 'old' ways of treating illness can usually be disregarded.

However, uniquely, this isn't the case in Martial Arts where some modern styles like MMA are criticised for their lack of history and in turn integrity. This simply doesn't make sense in the grand scheme of things. Modern styles have evolved as the threats we face have evolved. If anything the older, very traditional styles should perhaps look to the modern developments in self-defence to adapt their Art to the world of today.

The early founders of each martial art were obviously at the beginning of its development, they were still learning. Despite the manner in which they are now respected, they could not have known in the beginning where their systems would go. It would have been impossible for them to foresee distant generations looking for answers. They were too busy trying to live their lives and prevent the neighbouring village from plundering their home/livestock/wives.

The founders of Martial Arts weren't gods or saints, but real, ordinary men and women. They worked with skill and instinct, but not magic. Perhaps they made wise observations, but that doesn't mean their answers would apply to combat thousands of years AFTER their lifetimes.

Similar to self-defence, astrology for example, has been practiced since near the dawn of time. Without meteorologists or maps, the skies and stars were the only oracles to follow. Despite thousands of years of practice astrology's vast resource of knowledge is now cast aside as fairly useless. Sure it can be fun to dive into one's horoscope, or try to divine the best choice by consulting the planets, but in reality it's almost strictly a source of entertainment in the modern world. Its time has passed.

If a businessman looked to the stars for guidance regarding important corporate decisions most people would think he was crazy, and yet thousands of students every day learn detailed and bizarre forms or Kata movements that have very little regard to realistic and practical self-defense.

Perhaps then it's simply that people *want* to believe in the mysticism of Martial Arts, something all the more difficult when a style's entire history is documented clearly on Wikipedia. Traditional styles however mix fact, fiction and legend into an enticing theatrical package; a package the organisations running these arts are quick to embrace.

Ultimately older arts are simply a different approach to training; by encompassing history, philosophy and ancient concepts of combat rather than purely effective ones. As students, if we are conscious of these differences and choose to embrace them, then traditional styles are just as valid as modern ones.

The "Best" Martial Art of All

Which one Martial Art could be considered the 'best'?

The most popular argument against time travel is that we haven't met any time travellers. Similarly the most popular argument against one Martial Art being 'the best' is that we aren't all getting our backsides kicked on a daily basis by the master of this style.

Among the highly opinionated world of combat arts one of the biggest on-going arguments is whether 'X' style is better than 'Y'. Students who have dedicated many years of practise to one system or another are of course protective of the time and perhaps financial investments they have made and many are vocal about how their brand of Martial skills is best.

Across Self-Defense applications, tournament wins, striking power, grappling prowess and many other measures could one style be considered the all-round most effective style? Such a question cannot be answered by armchair debates, but that begs another inquiry: how do we test it?

Naturally a competition between two styles would be the most obvious method of comparison. Few tournaments exist that include one pure style vs. another but the early days of Mixed Martial Arts offered the chance for participants to test their mettle against other styles.

In the 1990's, the UFC and similar competitions allowed the opportunity for people of different martial arts to directly compete against each other in much more specific arts, (compared to today where most fighters cross-train in multiple styles).

In these early days it was the Gracie family who shocked the world by defeating much bigger opponents of other styles with a form of ground fighting not commonly seen at the time. This of course was the Gracie form of Brazilian Jujitsu – now a popular worldwide art.

So is Gracie Jujitsu the winner here?

In one simple world, 'no', because their techniques, though devastating, were simply effective for that arena at that time. You may assume that perhaps then Gracie Jujitsu was the best in that era, even if it might not be now. But again it is not quite so simple. If we take a look at the rules of the competition it becomes apparent that the UFC style matches actually favoured ground fighters once combat went to the floor, since strikers suddenly found many of the most effective techniques against the rules. The same is true even today;

1. *Striking downward using the point of the elbow*
2. *Striking to the spine or the back of the head*
3. *Kicking to the kidney with a heel*
4. *Throat strikes of any kind, including, without limitation, grabbing the trachea*

- All banned in the UFC arena.

Sure, these are nasty techniques and prohibiting them makes sense for the long term health of all fighters but if you specialise in striking, I.e. only hitting someone, then once a grappler is attempting some kind of lock or hold you cannot use any of the most powerful techniques that would work in a self-defense or 'real' fight scenario, basically favouring the grappler.

Does this prove that Brazilian Jujitsu is a better style? In this circumstance perhaps, but widely? Not so much.

Even fan favorites like Anderson Silva and Fedor Emelianenko are known to have combined elements from many different disciplines to be successful. If one art was all-conquering we can assume it would be the mainstay of not just all combat sports but combat in general.

Secret Dominance

So what about a potentially secret caste of Martial Arts elite, could they triumph over the rest of us? Could there be hidden masters, even now, that have the knowledge and ability to beat all other styles, yet prefer to remain in hiding?

Rumours abound of rare Shaolin feats and remote gurus that could decimate other combatants with exotic techniques never before seen. You may have come across the odd video on Youtube or heard of such marvels through other students.

While knowledge is indeed power, it seems that practical, not mystical, training might be a bit more convincing in this case. When those with the most influence (wealthy citizens and political policy-makers) begin to feel threatened it is unlikely that they would worry about kicks, jabs, or Kiai mind control. The influential and the affluent are experts at protecting their interests and as yet there are no accounts of a Diplomat employing a local Karate school for close protection. Bodyguards and security specialists are typically trained in a mix of Street-ready and purely practical combat techniques. If there was one secret style to dominate all others they would know about it.

But what if the same network existed in ancient times could they have defeated all other styles? This theory may hold a little more water. In the past, weapons were simpler, and a martial artist would certainly have a better chance of getting close enough to a target to inflict their intentions. Yet over the supposed thousands of years that Martial Arts have existed in various forms, they have failed to make a difference in any notable regimes aside from perhaps the Shaolin influence in overthrowing Wang Shichong, a Chinese General and self-declared emperor in the Sui Dynasty around 621AD. Even then the influence was local however.

This whole idea of world or even stylistic domination via the mystical knowledge of Martial Arts seems increasingly impossible. Or maybe it is a just a marketing ploy to entice new recruits?

Not quite ready to give up on the dream? Perhaps we are taking this concept of 'the best' a bit too literally. Maybe we have missed an important nuance because the true meaning was lost in translation a few hundred years ago. Maybe the intended suggestion here is simply that there is a 'best' style for you and you alone. We all learn and respond in different ways and finding an Art that resonates 'best' with you will yield the 'best' results

After all if someone who has studied Judo for 10 years beats someone who has practised Karate for 2 months it doesn't mean Judo is better. Merely that the practitioner has more experience and responded better to that style. This is what it ultimately comes down to; personal engagement.

No one style has all the answers or techniques but if you fully embrace the challenges and experiences of any Martial Art you will be far more able and skilled than an individual who is merely going through the motions of attending each week. After all, why set out to conquer the world when happiness lies in simply conquering yourself?

How to Choose the 'Best' Martial Art for YOU

So, as we've learned, the 'best' martial art is probably the one that you respond to most successfully but how do you choose where to start? With the myriad styles available and organizations working overtime to recruit new students it can be hard to pick a direction.

One simple way is to consider what type of learner you are. If you remember back to your school days, or any recent education what type of class did you respond best to?

Organised and disciplined: You enjoy rigid lesson plans, knowing what will happen each time and find remembering facts and figures easy.

You should try: Traditional Arts like Karate, Kung Fu, Aikido, Taekwondo and more.

The structured learning and classroom hierarchy will feel familiar and you will find the patterns and terminology easy to remember. You will also appreciate the precision and attention to detail traditional arts require.

Freeform and Unstructured: You prefer working in small groups or with others in a relaxed and unstructured format

You Should Try: Modern styles like Krav Maga, reality based self defense or Cross Training workshops

Although many modern styles may still include belts and gradings they are usually more relaxed and adaptive in format to reflect real self-defense requirements. Typically you will find it beneficial to work with a partner and learn at your own pace.

Short Attention Span / Physical Learner: You find it hard to remember things and follow plans but find yourself focused and able to put in great effort when moving around, running or using your hands.

You should try: Physically intensive arts like Muay Thai, MMA or even boxing.

Physical learners really come into their own when pushing their body to the limit. Where most people would struggle under intense physical demand you become more focused and develop technique through muscle memory, rather than just mental discipline.

Always try out a Martial Art before committing to it, even if it looks perfect on paper. Your personal response to training will make the difference between a flash-in-the-pan fad or a lifetime of physical and mental benefits.

Pressure Points and the Touch of Death

Can deadly pressure points really work?

It is easy to dismiss the idea of deadly touches as ridiculous. Or is it?

A quick search online reveals multiple videos of so-called Masters demonstrating a killer, yet incredibly mysterious and gentle, touch that incapacitates the opponent within seconds. Could there be truth to the legend?

The touch of death or even touch of paralysis is a technique typically featured in films, books and more often anecdotes. (A friend of a friend training in a club one town over told me about this technique). It usually involves a tiny movement or slight touch to some part of the body which completely incapacitates the enemy.

As you'd expect there is little scientific evidence of such a technique working in real life, but is there some truth to the legend?

In case you are still under the spell, let's just start out by stating that just because something occurs in a movie does not mean it is realistic. Production teams use special effects for a reason. If it was as simple as filming a real-live event then people would be uploading visual proof for all to see. Movie makers exist to make us believe what we see, and some of them are very good at it. It's hugely entertaining but it is fictional – no matter how realistic it appears.

Even quasi-accurate films or those 'based on a true story' are manipulated to appear and sound more believable.

For anyone who has not heard of this legend, the idea is that certain Martial Arts masters can develop a special skill to kill another individual with a simple tap. In different versions they may also be afforded the ability to determine whether or not their adversary will die as a result of such actions. Finally there is yet another outrageous claim that one can develop a kind of touch that burns the opponents skin, leaving a scar and eventually contributing to their death much later after the fact.

It should be said that I've met some severely pissed-off and ignorant people over the years, and if this ability was really possible there is no doubt that they would be all over this brand of insta-kill. With myths like these it is easier to understand some people's disdain for being touched at all.

Such a legend also benefits the more elderly Martial Arts masters. What better way to keep adversaries at bay and improve reputation than by perpetuating a myth to instill fear or admiration? And what better way for the Sifu/Sensei to get out of sparring (and therefore ever having to prove they actually KNOW anything) than by saying it's "too dangerous?" Even if you have the common sense to doubt such a power, would you be willing to risk being wrong?

Your kindly old Kung Fu instructor may be 98 years old but you *somehow* know he could take you to school.

So how did this odd 'touch of death' concept get started anyway? Most people trace this legend straight to the power source of most Martial Arts systems. In ancient China the theory began that a substance known as 'Qi', or 'Chi', flows throughout a person's body affecting everything from strength and vitality to illnesses and personality. In fact the concept of Chi continues even today among most of modern China, influencing architecture and design (Feng Shui), Martial Arts and even healthcare. According to proponents of traditional Chinese Medicine Chi is the energy force of life.

Note the word "Force" in there. Any film fans again might recognize parallels with another esoteric group of warrior monks from the big screen. The concept of Qi is far reaching and influential even today. Although abstract, the Qi essence has led to numerous philosophies and healing systems.

This energy is thought to flow through fourteen meridians or channels. One might picture this much like the blood that flows through our veins, except Chi and its channels are invisible to the eye. Good flow of energy means that one experiences good health on a holistic level. Blocked or imbalanced flow however can have negative effects on one's lifestyle, personality, and health.

Qi is an interesting concept being that it doesn't truly exist in the sparkly magic land of unicorns and fat-free pizza you are likely imagining. After all, living things certainly have some sort of spark, a sentience to differentiate between animate beings and inanimate objects but to truly understand this topic we must consider the situation in ancient China. The Qi theory predates modern miracles like microscopes and the discovery of the cell or any scientific understanding of organ function. The body itself was a mysterious, magical, thing. Qi was as good a way as any to describe the source of life.

Where polarity theory seeks to treat ailments by unblocking or redirecting the currents of Chi, or acupuncture may stimulate it with needles, a martial artist might attempt to conquer their opponent by manipulating their Chi. Of course these three systems lack one thing: efficacy. There is no way to prove the result because Qi (Chi) cannot be measured or seen. A participant may feel different, but there is certainly cause to consider the potential of a placebo effect, which is proven to often be quite beneficial and healing in itself.

While acupuncture is seen as a healing modality, 'Dim Mok' or the 'Touch of Death' exists as its opposite. The concept is similar, but the practitioner manipulates Chi towards imbalance in order to subdue or harm an opponent. A master is said to affect someone using solely the powers of thought and intention. The supposed touch of death relies on adept manipulations to touch at just the right point to stop the flow of chi, or life energy.

Can modern understandings of anatomy back up the plausibility of Dim Mok? Ancient Chinese medicine and modern medicine agree that there are points on the body where energy flows more than others. You might know these as pressure points. They form in areas where the nerves lie close to skin, making them more accessible. You may have experienced a jolt of discomfort as friend or acupressure specialist has squeezed or pressed one of these points.

While debate rages about the science behind the practice of energy modalities like Acupuncture some recent studies have shown a physiological difference between bodily tissues in certain 'acupressure' spots on the body

A recent study published in the JOURNAL OF ELECTRON SPECTROSCOPY REVEALED THAT SOME ACUPUNCTURE SPOTS ON THE BODY CONTAIN A *"higher density of micro-vessels and contain a large amount of involuted microvascular structures".* DOES THIS PROVE CHI MERIDIANS EXIST? NOT FOR ME TO SAY, BUT THE HUMAN BODY DOES CERTAINLY VARY IN COMPOSITION THROUGHOUT CERTAIN AREAS.

It is easy to demonstrate that the body can be stimulated in these locations with interesting and sometimes profound effects. So could pressing these points cause death? If one of these points were subject to a hefty blow then there is a potential for damage, perhaps a momentary loss of consciousness. If the nerves were stimulated to the point of irritating the brain into turning off for a moment then the heart might also stop.

In the myth however, we are not talking about a blow with considerable force, which we all know could cause damage and even death but a deft flick of technique with the correct "intention".

In reality a light touch, no matter how carefully applied is extremely unlikely to finish someone off. The nerves at the back of the neck, which directly control the blood within the heart and brain, might seem like the best candidates. However, like most bodily locations these are well protected for evolutionary reasons and would take much more than a tap to infiltrate.

Even if such a skill were legitimate, it would not be possible to perfect it to the extent of finding that magic point on anyone in just a matter of moments. Don't forget that everybody is different. Though the basic structure might be the same, we come in all shapes and sizes. Varying amounts of muscles and fat get in the way of nerves therefore, you might be surprised to learn that they are not necessarily located at the exact same spot from one person to the next. In extreme cases even organs are located in different places from one person to the next.

The way each of us responds to stimuli varies as well. In a group of five, one person might laugh, while another cries, and the third passes out, while the remaining two might have no reaction at all.

The real question is if such a skill did exist, how would one practice enough to become a master of the death touch? There cannot be too many people lining up to be guinea pigs for this particular experiment. (Despite that Ad I ran on Craigslist)

Though a rather handy defence tool, it could only be practiced by one with truly malicious intent since every time you wanted to brush up on the skill, someone would have to die or become paralysed. It's hardly practical running around killing random people in the name of perfecting your special Martial Arts skill. Not to mention that you would find yourself leading a lonely existence. Even the truest of friends aren't likely to stick around when each innocent handshake found them fearing for their lives. Even if it were remotely plausible, the touch of death clearly has no real place in any relatively peaceful society.

Ultimately pressure points work but only with significant effort. They aren't an instant end to any conflict but they can be seen as a bonus target for a strike.

Lightly touching your annoying work colleague's knee, no matter how much you want them to die, is less likely to finish them off and more likely to involve a visit from HR.

How to Test Your Own Pressure Point Tolerance

Bring one hand out in front of your body so that the palm is directed toward the floor. Now with the thumb and forefinger of the other hand locate the spot on the first hand where the base of your thumb bone meets that of your wrist. Squeeze the pressure point that lies just before this juncture. Begin with a mild squeeze to test your reaction. If it isn't too intense try again with a slightly stronger hold.

Pressure Points You Can Use

Dismissing the obvious and more well-known 'pressure points' such as Eye gouges or kicks to the groin there exists numerous points of weakness on the human body that can be exploited for self-defense purposes.

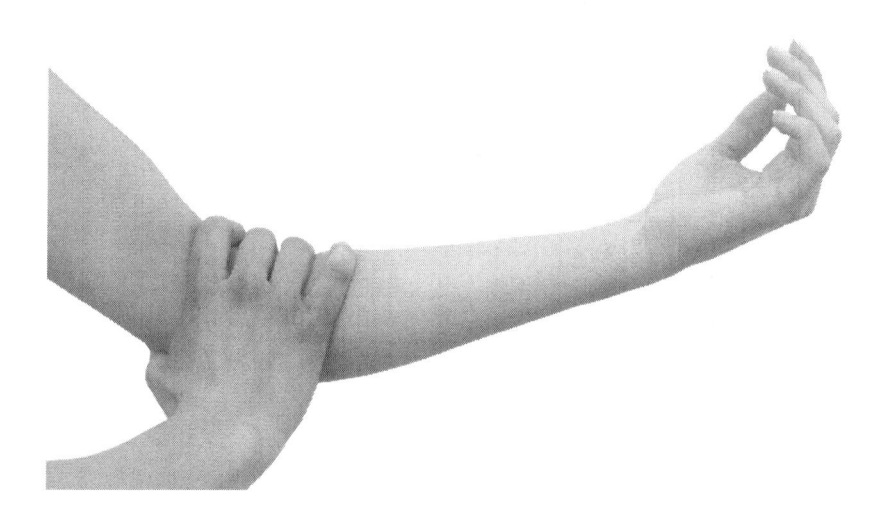

Essentially these are areas where high blood flow runs close to the surface or nerves are especially unprotected. Even so a gentle touch will do little. Pressure points are basically a bonus to the bigger movements you might make to protect yourself. If you can jam a thumb or finger in you might create enough pain to give yourself chance to escape. A gentle prod however is more likely to annoy an opponent than incapacitate them.

- **Clavicle**

Sometimes called 'Hichu' within Japanese Martial Arts this is where the neck joins the chest in middle between the collar bones. You can push a thumb in here for self defense.

- **Inner Elbow**

Known as 'Kote' this point the inside part of the elbow and can be utilised with a strike to inflict pain or restrict blood flow.

- **Philtrum**

Where the nose meets the lips is a particularly sensitive area that can be easily affected with a strike.

- **Hand Webbing**

Where the thumb joins to the first finger is a fleshy area. This spot has long been popular in both healing and Martial Arts practices for hundreds of years. Pressure here can be applied hard and fast for defense purposes.

To find out more check out how to use Pressure Points in my best selling Self Defense book: 'Self Defense Made Simple'

Martial Arts Superpowers

How much of what we hear and see about the legendary abilities of Martial Artists is true?

We all know that there are some talented individuals out there. Many of us may have become involved in Martial Arts due to the incredible feats of speed, strength or endurance we have witnessed in person or on the screen but are these skills possible for anyone to achieve or are they reserved for the athletic elite and Martial Arts Superhumans?

The legend of supernatural combat techniques is regularly perpetuated in Martial Arts films, video games, and TV. They somewhat innocently confuse Martial Arts with an interesting mix of gymnastics and super powers. I say innocently because it's unlikely that the goal is to lie to the public so much as it is to create an entertaining experience and get more viewers.

The jumps that vault a Kung Fu master twenty feet in the air, allowing him to suspend long enough to do three somersaults, and four lethal kicks before landing upright are nothing short of incredible. They are also largely physically impossible. This fact should seem as obvious as the wires and harnesses they use to perform those stunts. Still, there are always a few who actually believe they can do this stuff.

Perhaps then it is our fault for taking what we see on screen as attainable. Or is it?

After all, editing has become rather impressive in recent years with computer generated graphics and millions of dollars spent on the average blockbuster movie. Budgets and effects were not quite as compelling in the days of Bruce Lee. (But we'll get to him in due time…)

Was it Wushu?

However, could it be 'Wushu' responsible for creating the biggest illusions within the world of Martial Arts entertainment?

As a term 'Wushu' generally defines the various Chinese Martial Arts and is interchangeable with 'Kung Fu' depending on where you are in the world, but Wushu as a Martial Art, is today a style all of its own and one that includes a great element of exhibition aiming to make combatants appear skilful and flowing.

Developed post World War 2 the style found its feet in the early fifties and was established in an effort to standardise the myriad Chinese arts under the communist government. Over time two main elements emerged, 'Sanda' or Chinese Kickboxing and 'Taolu' or forms. Taolu especially is quite beautiful and spectacular to watch, encouraging exquisite displays of balance, form, speed and gymnastics.

Is it effective in self-defense? Probably not, but it looks so good that the style soon caught the eye of movie producers and before long fight choreographers and directors were drafting in Martial Artists skilled at this craft to make the combat in their movies look more spectacular.

Wushu masters dedicate their entire lives to making such movements look effortless and flowing, leading many to assume that the techniques they perform are easy to achieve for any martial artist. The truth is that like any skill the acrobatic movements of advanced Taolu are indeed possible but require years of practise and in fact are more closely tied to gymnastic and even circus skills than Martial Arts.

While Wushu as a discipline might be fairly modern it is not to be confused with 'Wuxia' – or the traditional stories of Martial Arts heroes. In China these folk tales have existed for millennia and might be seen as equivalent to the heroic yarns involving knights, dragons and damsels in Europe. As with any legend these stories have today been brought to the big screen, video games and other media.

If that wasn't confusing enough, the heroes of Wuxia tales often use Wushu techniques to save the day. Little wonder then that so many people grow up wanting to learn these fantastical techniques – even if they are a mix of acrobatics and fantasy.

There are of course many skills that can be acquired through Martial Arts. There is confidence, strength, self-awareness, agility and speed, and even plenty of impressive spinning jumping techniques. These all lend themselves to an effective defence in that style. However, they are also all limited by good old fashioned physics.

How high you can jump, how fast you can move, and the amount of time you remain in the air are limited by your size, weight, proficiency, and of course gravity. The relationship between these variables can open up a world of possibilities.

For starters, no matter how strong you may become there is no way to develop enough human strength to launch into the air any higher than maybe 8 or so feet. At a roughly equivalent 2.45 meters, a highly practiced Cuban by the name of Javier Sotomayor is, at time of writing, the only person to ever clear eight feet in height and even this was only done twice by him, a long time ago.

It should be noted that his achievement sets the standard for the world and was not established easily. It took many years of hard work and dedication and this record has not been beaten (at time of going to press) despite nearly a century of attempts by fellow athletes. The highest female jump has remained at 2.09 meters since 1987. It seems that humans have met their ceiling in this regard. Legends alleging 20, 30, or even 40 foot leaps are sadly fallacious and all the training in the world is unlikely to budge the record much.

Even the rigorous training of martial artists cannot top the impossible. We leave that to the X-Men. Though perhaps in a class of their own as far as pushing limits, martial artists cannot surpass the arithmetic. If it were possible, we would all be doing it. Who wouldn't enjoy a Saturday afternoon bouncing, swirling, and hovering around the park? (Without the use of illegal drugs).

Masters of any superhuman skills might be instructed to keep them under wraps but somewhere someone would have sold out their ability for a little media attention. There would be pictures and videos. We do not live in an age where secrets stay hidden for long. We are nosy and voyeuristic by nature, a fact easily proven by the latest celebrity headlines, and further demonstrated by the popularity of reality television.

If leaping over sky scrapers is out of the question for non-Kryptonians, is it possible to move with lightning speed, so fast it seems as though one is defying the laws of motion? Some martial artists certainly seem to develop a super human quickness and agility when it comes to performing those sequences... which they have no doubt practiced a hundred times before. Though note that faster does not always correlate with accuracy and there are still limiting factors. Martial Arts masters of WuShu for example, are in fact typically asked to perform in slow motion for better visibility on the big screen.

So far the fastest speed at which an individual can run has been established at about 100 meters in 10 seconds. That's pretty quick, but not easily accomplished by the average person. Smaller, muscular people tend to be faster than those with larger builds based solely on the laws of physics. A larger mass will take more time and energy to reach the same momentum as a smaller, lighter mass. Of course anyone can increase their speed with repetition, though those near the maximum speed will see smaller increases as their skills level off with reality.

Endurance is another interesting concept exaggerated in movies. In real life very few physical conflicts last five minutes or longer, most being resolved in under Ten seconds. Regardless of skill level most fighters want the battle over as fast as possible to avoid injury. If a fight were to last the 10 minutes they do on Screen both parties would likely be a mess of broken bones and brain damage. Either that or they would get bored and quit!

Of course, a ten second knockout doesn't fill the seats with paying customers in the same way. Just watch a clip of a fast knockout in a high profile boxing bout and see the crowd reaction when they realise the match is over in under a minute and their ringside seats are now expensive coat racks.

Practice makes perfect

Ultimately Martial Artists are limited by physics just like everyone else. No surprise there perhaps, but the real skill may be in becoming adept at such a wide range of abilities. Having the speed to move fast, the strength to deliver a punch and the flexibility to deliver spectacular kicks makes for incredible viewing.

Some Martial Artists have also honed specific skills to the point of seeming almost heroic. There are no supernatural powers in effect here, just years and years of practice and hard work.

Like the man who catches arrows out of the air with his bare hands.

No really. World Record holder Anthony Kelly was able to snatch 33 arrows clean out of the air as they were fired at full speed from a genuine bow in less than 2 minutes. You can view this remarkable feat in numerous videos online.

Mystical abilities or years of training and great reflexes?
You decide.

Almost Everything You Know About Ninjas

Few things in life are as cool as Ninjas. The mystery, the deadly skills, the sneaky weapons; little wonder then that they hold such a beloved place within popular culture.

Today Ninjitsu as a Martial Art is still practiced by many dedicated students, even if it is not necessarily popular compared to the numbers involved in Karate or Taekwondo. Grandmaster Masaaki Hatsumi is regarded by most as the modern father of this ancient and stealthy style heading up 'Bujinkan' which employs locks, holds, hidden weapons and dirty fighting.

So it sounds pretty much like the films then.

Ok, we all know that movies, even those based on Historical events, can use liberal amounts of artistic license (I'm looking at you William Wallace), but the concept of black-clad Ninja assassins is so thoroughly ingrained in the history of Martial Arts and Japanese warfare that most of us rarely question if it was true and with modern practitioners still embracing the ideals of stealthy assassins it is difficult to imagine it any other way.

Even pseudo-accurate films like The Last Samurai depict Ninjas as midnight-clad death dealers, prowling rooftops and kicking some upper-class backside.

But Actually…

Ninjas were just like you and me. Or at least you and me in 15th Century Japan. They looked like everyone else. Used 'normal' weapons or indeed anything they could get their hands on and almost certainly didn't wear black.

One of the biggest misconceptions around the Ninja is around their definition. While many may assume it focuses on killing enemies or secret weapons the actual meaning is derived from the term 'Shinobi' – which you may have heard. While this phrase doesn't directly translate into one single phrase in English the general meaning is a combination of *Stealth*, *hiding* and *escape by any means*.

The lesson here is that the Shinobi focused on evasion and observation, not outright combat or even using weapons. Their tenets ensuring that they blended in with the populace.

Ninjas may have existed as early as the Eleven hundreds but developed as an organized force of mercenaries, spies and killers for hire within the 15th, 16th and 17th Century . They undertook nasty and difficult tasks for those that could afford their services. As such it was important that they could blend in and adapt to any situation.

In fact Ninjas, or Shinobi often took on the opposite role of the Samurai. While the Samurai were bound by strict honor codes and laws the Ninja were free to get the job done in any manner they saw fit.

Because of this improvised approach the many stereotypes surrounding their activities become all the more spurious.

The Weapons

Modern Ninjistu training through Bujinkan is much like traditional Ninjitsu in that numerous different weapons are used and numerous different weapons are trained against. Not all are/were used purely for attack or defense with many being employed for distraction or evasion only.

Most people also think the Ninja used their own unique blade or 'Ninjato' in their trade. Typically this resembles a straight version of a Katana but interestingly most research indicates this is a modern fabrication since no evidence exists of this type of sword ever being used. More likely the Ninja, masters of adaptation, would utilize whatever was to hand and trained with Samurai Katana, daggers and even simple farming tools. Besides, carrying around a uniquely Shinobi weapon wouldn't exactly be stealthy for the undercover saboteur.

Perhaps equally famous is the 'Shuriken', sometimes called the 'throwing star'. Far from flinging death to enemies from 20ft away Shurikens were actually used as a backup blade in close encounters or at a push for throwing as a distraction only to aid in escape. They were designed to slash and slice but not to kill by hurling from afar.

Shuriken also took numerous forms. Not all of which were star shaped or symmetrical. Some were short blades or weighted knives for ease of transport.

Back in Black

Even in the unlikely scenario of a midnight rooftop assault black would be a poor color choice for outfits and again no evidence exists suggesting Ninja used a specific outfit.

Despite what you might think Black actually sticks out against the evening sky. Modern soldiers use patterns based around dark blues and greys – much closer to the natural tone of outdoor darkness.

Think about it, if you saw a guy in full military camouflage wandering through your town he would stick out like a sore thumb but if the same individual dressed like everyone else you wouldn't look twice. The same was true of Ninja who may have used dark clothing but would have dressed like local peasants or farmers to blend in.

The Three Schools of Training

The 'Iga-ryū' or 'Iga School' of Ninjistu is regarded by many as the most famed sources of classical Ninjistu training in its time. Their three main areas of focus demonstrate the skills of the Ninja:

Toiri-no-jutsu – This area of teaching focused on abilities outside of open warfare and the patience and preparation involved in achieving a goal – usually by sneaking into a location, long-term undercover work, subterfuge or use of contacts to infiltrate a secure compound. It emphasized the 'long game' in achieving the Ninja's goal, be it ultimately assassination, sabotage or surveillance.

Chikairi-no-jutsu – This part of the school centered on skills during battle and open warfare, in particular the infiltration of the enemy ranks and movement behind enemy lines in order to disrupt troops or sabotage supplies and weapons.

Ongyo-jutsu – The final specialty was the most famous; escape. Here the Ninja learned to 'escape by any means'. This training typically employed both 'hiding' and 'disappearing'. Ninjitsu practitioners became so skilled at using distractions or 'tricks' to evade capture that legends developed regarding their ability to vanish into thin air or turn into shadows.

The truth of course is that unbound by the strict code of the Samurai a Ninja could, and would use dirty fighting, unethical tactics and camouflage to achieve their goal. At a time when the nobility may have seemed far from reach of the common people the legend of powerful, yet down-to-earth heroes would have spread fast. Like an Asian Robin Hood the reputation of the Ninja took on elements of both truth and fantasy as it spread across the world.

Today we can take much of what we hear with a pinch of salt but the truth behind the legend becomes, as is often the case, just as interesting.

The Legendary Samurai Sword

Few weapons within the Martial Arts lexicon are as famous as the Samurai Sword. Beautiful, deadly and forged with unrivaled precision they are even today an item to be envied and have a powerful reputation as the best blades in existence.

But is this reputation deserved?

Firstly let's take a look at just what a 'Samurai Sword' is.

While many people use the term for any blade of similar shape a 'Katana' is the traditional sword of the Samurai that gained notoriety during the feudal days of Japan. It is of 'standard' length with moderate curvature – different to the more traditional curved 'Tachi' of older eras.

In fact the length of such a Japanese blade determines what category it falls into. Katanas are defined as 'standard' length, typically meaning over 606mm or a 'long sword'. Many people mistake the shorter versions as also Katanas but these fall into other categories too, with the 'Wakizashi' being between 300 and 600mm and 'Tanto' being the 'short blade' of the bunch measuring up as more of a dagger or knife, around 150-300mm. Though all are technically 'Samurai Swords' the Katana is generally considered the blade of fame.

- Katana – Over 606mm in length
- Wakizashi – 300 – 600mm
- Tanto – 150 – 300mm

The three blades also often held places next to each other, being suited to different environments. It was common for Samurai to carry two swords or 'daisho'; with a full size Katana being accompanied by a Wakizashi or Tanto depending on requirements. After-all, fighting indoors around narrow corridors, tables and chairs would be near impossible with a full-sized sword.

The Ikea spares department would make a fortune.

Why the fame?

As always movies and TV have a lot to answer for regarding the fame of the Katana. Kill Bill, 47 Ronin, heck even the Ninja Turtles depicted the use of these legendary weapons. But what specifically is supposed to be so great about them?

"Samurai Swords were crafted over thousands of hours by folding the steel – making it stronger than any equivalent blade."

That may sound awesome but there is a reason Japanese swordsmiths 'folded' the steel so many times. The process is used to remove impurities, in particular Carbon, from the metal.

The Japanese metal workers of that time often utilized a product known in Europe as 'Pig Iron'. It wasn't that European Smiths couldn't work this material, it was that they thought it was so poor it wasn't worthy of forging.

Despite its prevalence now Steel was not easy to come across in ancient times. It was common for old or broken swords to be melted down and re-forged. Even the weapons or steel tools of the enemy were fair game for re-shaping.

Because of this mix of metal quality and potentially high Carbon content 'folding' was required by Japanese Smiths to bring steel-based weapons up to standard. It didn't make the blades superior, it simply made them usable.

"Katanas were so sharp they could cleave through Bone, Metal or anything stupid enough to get close"

Contrary to popular belief swordfights in any battle rarely involved clanging blade edges against each other with sparks flying everywhere because this would ruin the weapon or shatter the blade faster than you can say 'Zatoichi'.

Katanas were no different in this regard and users trained to aim for the gaps in armor or weak points of the body. Even with this knowledge use of a Katana is highly specialized if you don't want to damage the sword.

Today numerous specialist collectors and enthusiasts practice the old styles and seek to understand traditional Katana use. (Hopefully just for posterity's sake!) Even with modern knowledge and training the slightest misuse of the Samurai sword can lead to the blade shattering along with the wielders dreams of sword ownership.

Entire books exist regarding the precise use of the blade and videos abound of today's users getting the angle 'slightly' wrong, completely destroying the weapon. The Katana is indeed a tricky thing to master and certainly don't cut through everything.

"Japanese Samurai Swords were better than anything in the West"

Of course most Martial Artists start drooling at the mere sight of a true-forged Katana and its appearance in Feudal Japan was quite different to anything being used in Europe at the same time.

Naturally the conclusion became that these mysterious islanders had created a sword of the gods, unrivalled elsewhere. The reality is that swords were being created all over the place that were stronger, sharper and easier to use – if not quite as exotic.

For example when the European knights crusaded their way into the Middle East they came across an incredibly sharp steel never before seen.

They christened it 'Damascus Steel' due to its location and presumably because they were too busy fighting to come up with something more creative.

Damascus Steel remained a mystery for many years until Stanford University researchers recently claimed to have cracked the formula, but even now it is difficult to recreate. Yet Middle-Eastern Smiths engineered these superior blades long before the Samurai started using the Katana.

Perhaps then the legendary status of the 'Samurai Sword' is less about pure battle-effectiveness and more about their role within Martial History. Their unique and quite beautiful design the result of hundreds of hours of work.

While European Smiths churned out blades by the dozen the Japanese craftsman would have truly dedicated his life to creating objects of desire and destruction from less than ideal conditions – something far more impressive.

Combine this with their unique connection to Asian martial arts and they make a fine, if not quite world beating, addition to any Martial Artist's collection.

Bulletproof Monks and Martial Toughness

Can the best Martial Artists take more punishment than the rest of us?

The concept of partially indestructible Martial Artists is one closely tied to superhuman abilities as explored in a previous chapter.

There is a popular idea that certain masters of Martial Arts, as often demonstrated by the famed Shaolin Monks, are able to withstand pain or injury above and beyond that of the ordinary mortal. Somewhere someone got the idea that these special people can take a blow without the slightest hint of discomfort. But is this true, and if so how?

The mental training involved in Martial Arts might make the individual emotionally tougher, and better able to control their reactions, but on paper it does not reduce the ability of a blow to break a nose or crack a rib. (Believe me, I know…) After all, bones lack the ease at which muscles can be built and strengthened but there are some ways a student can improve resistance.

Again it comes down to physics. Skin can only withstand so much force before bruising or tearing, and a sharp sword will pierce it along with any internal organs it meets. Sure, skin that has become tough from hard work or a seasoned coating of calluses might slow a weapon by a few microseconds, but it will not coat the body like armour. Who has not gotten a few nicks from a kitchen knife or menacing bit of paper? A sharpened sword is hardly a comparison.

The famous Shaolin demonstrations of balancing on swords or cutting watermelons on an individual's chest are usually just precise examples of control and practise. Onlookers marvel at their impenetrable skin when in reality they should be amazed at the skill it takes to balance or hold a blade in the one spot where it won't slice through the body.

The magic of Hollywood might paint their heroes as able to resist sharpened edges, but even martial artists are human beings with inherent vulnerabilities. They are made of muscle and sinew not Adamantium or steel. Some theorize that stronger muscles might become one's armour. However, no muscle is going to get strong or dense enough to stand up to a blade or excessive blunt force.

But beyond resisting weapons it is possible to improve overall toughness for self-defense. One example is the development of muscles to protect sensitive areas in a fall. The back is a great demonstration of this and back raising exercises build the Erector Spinae Muscles around the spine reduces the chance of direct impact damage to the sensitive Spinous Processes.

Another theory points to the opposite extreme, suggesting that relaxation might be the key to becoming durable in the face of potential bodily harm. This isn't an entirely terrible theory. When muscles are relaxed they lose some of their density allowing a few extra centimetres space between one's body and the approaching force. It's also the reason why drunks don't seem to suffer so badly from falling over/into things, (stay off the booze though kids). While it can help, a small amount injury still occurs. It's simply not enough of an advantage to withstand the punishment we see in the movies.

Pain Tolerance

One thing about pain that IS true is that some of us are more responsive to pain than others. We all have differing levels of what we can physically endure before reacting. There is also a wide variance in the size and strength of each individual's build along with differences in how strong of a blow each of us may deliver. Many could certainly take a young child's strike without batting an eye. Being hit by an angry MMA champion is another story. Pain is subjective, both to the giver and receiver.

Just how much more can a dedicated martial artist at peak physical conditioning absorb beyond the limits of the average couch potato? As previously mentioned their muscles would provide an extra level of protection, akin to perhaps leather armour. These muscles can be a bit of a double edges sword though. Depending on the location of a blow, the pain may be cushioned before reaching the nerves nestled far below layers of muscles, or it could directly hit a muscle nerve inflicting severe pain from even a relatively weak impact.

Conditioning and the Iron Fist

Some martial artists train in a more realistic manner, by taking and serving thousands of repetitive blows, thrusting fists into vessels of sand or coarse gravel, or kicking wooden pillars with a light to moderate power. This is known as 'conditioning' and works by essentially letting the body adapt to the constant impact by building extraordinary thick skin and muscle. Individuals, who have grown accustomed to withstanding discomfort and developed 'tougher' skin, will have the ability to take more abuse as well as control their reactions to an attack.

Physically the areas receiving punishment will develop a kind of scar tissue adding an extra layer of buffering. This kind of conditioning can give the performer an edge. However there is also a thin line to navigate as such activities can deaden the nerves, extracting additional toughness but opening oneself up for future health concerns, loss of feeling, coordination, and agility if done to an excessive degree.

Practitioners of the unusual 'Iron Fist' Kung Fu for example, take conditioning to the extreme. If you've never heard of the style or seen their incredible exploits check out a few videos online and prepare to be in equal parts awed and horrified.

Iron Fist Kung Fu focuses on intense conditioning of the fist, (usually just the right since China, like many places, holds a strong cultural and sometimes superstitious bias against lefties). These individuals work for hours every week pummelling bags of gravel and sand to build up their hand and then treat them at the end of the day with Dit Da Jow – a traditional healing liniment.

And build it they do.

If you see any Iron Fist demonstrations around Beijing for example, you will see fellas with a swollen and rock-hard lump on the end of their right arm that resembles a hand after being run over in a cartoon.

The right apendage, about three times the size of the left, is also almost completely numb due to nerve damage and they use this to punch straight through blocks of concrete and wow onlookers by touching hot coals.

Incredible, but not exactly ideal for long term health.

Bones

Many people may assume that there is little that can be done to strengthen bones, aside from a healthy diet. While external conditioning might not work in the same way as say muscle or soft tissue numerous studies have examined which types of exercise are most beneficial, particularly for those suffering from skeletal conditions like Osteoporosis.

Traditionally resistance training has been promoted as the most useful in developing bone strength but a recent study from the University of Missouri actually discovered that while resistance training works, higher impact activity, like running, is actually more effective at strengthening bone tissue. Other research has also shown that exercise while younger leads to stronger bones in old age.

As a Martial Artist of course the easy way to train for higher impact activity, aside from running, is a healthy dose of jumping techniques, which put increased demand on the bones but in turn help them strengthen.

The Trick

The real skill of a trained martial artist is not in withstanding blows, but in blocking, deflection, and evasion. It is avoiding the kicks and punches of the opponent so that the full force of their strength never gains an opportunity to fall upon the defender anyway.

Sure, conditioning can and should be used to help improve resistance, both physically and mentally against impact but not taken to the extreme of losing function. Besides, many sensitive targets cannot be improved anyway.

Some areas of the body, such as the nose, back of the head, eyes and throat, cannot be trained to become stronger or immune to damage. In MMA circles these extra vulnerable body points, as we've previously mentioned are usually off limits – proof alone that we are unable to 'strengthen' these areas.

The story is more brutal on the streets where there are no rules. Here a fighter might lose some of his edge, but he can still excel with a sharp mind and quick reflexes. That is unless his opponent holds a knife or gun in his hand. No amount of training can overcome the limits of what a human can take. One cannot acquire enough muscle to stop a speeding bullet, absorb the power of a two by four, or deflect a sharp pointed object from impaling their skin.

There is only one way for a martial artist to survive an opponent with greater strength, superior training, a dirty fighting style, or arsenal of weapons. They must use their training to avoid the fight altogether.

The winner of a real fight is the one that walks away. By not getting involved in a conflict in the first place we cannot lose. This is perhaps the real secret of the indestructible warrior.

How You Can 'Toughen Up'

It's not just Martial Artists that benefit from increased pain and discomfort tolerance. Any athlete pushing his or her body to extremes will need to go beyond their 'comfort' zone to perform at the highest level.

Thankfully numerous sports coaches and experts have come up with several methods for increasing personal pain tolerance even if yours starts initially quite low. Always bear in mind that discomfort is a natural part of challenging your body but outright pain is not. If your pain scores above 7 out of 10 it is time to stop and avoid injury.

Slow Progression

The simplest method for increasing tolerance to pain is through gradual acceptance. If you go straight to your ultimate goal of punching a brick wall for example, you will fail quickly. Instead allow the body and mind time to adapt by increasing intensity over time.

The very best Martial Artists spend a little time every day working on conditioning in one form or another. If you are ever lucky enough to visit a Shaolin temple or Kung Fu School you will often find all the surrounding trees and nearby posts have finger and knuckle marks on them from the thousands of tiny strikes over the years.

- Start by getting the technique, say a finger strike, correct while not making any contact

- Then start striking a soft pad or mitt

- Move to striking a hard punch bag

- Step up to striking a specific conditioning device like a Makiwara (Karate), or gravel filled bag

- Finally start to strike something completely unyielding, a wall, a tree, wooden dummy etc.

Note that each of these steps should be undertaken over many months and repetition is key. The hardest aspect of conditioning can be boredom due to the repeated techniques. To make it easier set fixed goals each day for a number of techniques and ensure you get them done quickly though accurately.

The Secret to Breaking Boards

How do they break solid materials?

You've probably seen demonstrations of board or brick breaking within Martial Arts, and even those with no experience of training will be familiar with these attempts to destroy various 'solid' materials using only a hand or foot. But how does it really work? And is there a limit on what can be broken?

The practical use of breaking objects in Martial Arts is in theory to train participants how to focus their efforts for greater impact. It is also preached that if one can break a board, then they also have the capacity to break bones. Let's be honest - bones and boards are not equivalent materials but still, breaking things such as boards does take a practiced skill.

Newton's third law states that for every action there is an equal and opposite reaction. When an object is hit there a separate but opposite force which pushes back against the striker. In order to hit a board without breaking oneself, an individual must be able to endure an equal amount of force. Here lies the danger of trying to push beyond your physical limits. Mistakes tend to lead to broken bones.

Note that despite the bounds of modern technology, scientists have yet to develop any sort of shield which is able to fend off the opposing force described by Newton. There is no psychological skill or trick that can render an individual immune to these effects. It's our old friend Physics at work again. Thus, there are clear limits to the size and quantity of objects a martial artist can break. It is hard to measure an exact number as strength varies from one individual to the next. We can make some estimates though.

An average, dedicated and well-trained martial artist may initiate a force of about 3330N (Newtons) which might also be converted to 750 foot pounds. Depending on the size and thickness of a board, it will probably take between 1000N and 2000N to break. Some quick arithmetic shows that an average fighter could reasonably break two or three boards without meeting their limit.

An elite Martial Arts master, at the very peak of training, may have more power to deliver. A liberal guess might say that this martial artist might deliver three times the force of an amateur in a single blow. They would be both faster and have more strength. So maybe they can break six to nine boards. This feat is impressive, but nothing akin to the stacks of wood and concrete a hundred layers thick often associated with this myth.

Let's look at another instrument that is good at breaking through things. Could our martial artist's strike match the destruction of a speeding bullet? The secret to the power of a bullet is the speed at which it is fired from the gun. This is a simple concept to demonstrate. Simply throwing a few bullets at an opponent will do little harm, unless perhaps you are lucky enough to hit them square in the eye.

- The speed of a typical bullet levels at around 900 m/s (3240 kph).

- Compare this to the speed of an average individual's striking speed which reaches 2 m/s (45 kph)

- Our superior martial artist at perhaps 37.5 m/s (135 kph) – though this would be remarkable.

- The maximum destruction by a martial artist is then around 1/24th as powerful as a bullet. That is enough velocity to break through a few more physical barriers, but far from a truly destructive force demonstrated in even a slow bullet.

So far the discussion had focused on the breaking of wood. Wood is fairly solid, but does vary in strength due to variety and age. How about something stronger like concrete blocks? Again, you may have seen demonstrations of people cracking seemingly solid slabs or huge lumps of concrete. While it is possible to break a block or two, the same limitations are in place. No one can break an object unless there is a location in which the power needed to break the item is lower than the force necessary to break it.

Concrete especially provides a unique spectacle because of its appearance and composition. Concrete *looks* very strong, after all, buildings and roads are made from the stuff, but slightly alter the mixture with too much or too little cement or sand and you end up with weak, brittle and powdery material that falls apart at the first sign of a stiff breeze – let alone a strike. Since poorly mixed concrete is generally thrown out it is also the easiest type to find for demonstrations. Not all slabs or boards are poorly made of course, some are solid and near indestructible. The hard part is knowing which type you are dealing with.

Attempting to break something without intimate knowledge of the mechanisms in place will only result in injury. Most concrete blocks are actually narrower and therefore more vulnerable near the centre. A trained martial artist recognizes this venerable spot and uses it to their advantage. Similarly in breaking wooden boards I would advise striking along the grain, effectively exploiting a weakness within the material. The break still looks as impressive (which is usually the aim) but you don't end up in a sling for a month.

Ultimately remember that 'breaking' is fundamentally a demonstration, not a fighting technique. If we recognise the impressive spectacle it creates for onlookers and other students we can start to understand its important role within Martial Arts. Breaking has always been more of a showpiece and example than a genuine test of one's ability in combat.

How can I do it?

Breaking is as much about being smart as being tough. Strike hard and fast in the right area and most materials will weaken, if not break. However if you overlook even one small detail in the type of material, the board holder or target spot it is almost guaranteed you will end up with a sore hand and no break.

Breaking Essentials:

Holder must be rigid

If you are using another person to hold a board or plank it is absolutely crucial that they secure the board rigidly with no flex in the arms. It is instinctive for people to bend their elbows when they see an incoming strike but if this happens their arms will absorb all of the impact and despite your best efforts the board will remain mockingly intact.

Instead ensure they lock out their arms, keep the fingers away from the center and hold the board away from their face or groin – for obvious reasons!

Targeting

Precision is king with aiming to break boards. This is why the technique is usually only attempted by Black Belts or students of great experience – it requires perfect targeting.

Set yourself up slowly beforehand and closely examine your target while gauging the distance. When the time is right strike hard and fast to the center line of the board. If you are using wood ensure you strike along the grain, not against it.

Commitment

To break boards or blocks you need to clear your mind and become focused on the task at hand. Don't overthink things, worry about what might happen or get distracted by your surroundings. Just commit fully to striking through the target and do it.

Bonus Tip: Strikethrough

As an extra tip try to always imagine your target is 2 inches behind the actual board. This prevents 'drop-off'; where you subconsciously aim to only *just* hit the board.

By striking slightly *through* a target you are at peak power when you connect with the hand or foot. Aim to hit about 2 inches behind the material to ensure you go cleanly through it.

With practice, patience and keen observation a martial artist can break some materials but there is no secret power that allows them to break a hundred blocks stacked upon one another. This is not magic, but a focused and skilful manipulation of physics.

However, don't go out there thinking it is easy. As many have experienced in numerous demonstrations, it is absolutely crucial to hit the correct point in a perpendicular motion, at full power. Plus it takes years to practice the most effective techniques. Even with practice, there is no ancient wisdom that can overcome the laws of the universe. Everyone can break things, but only some have the finesse to shatter solid objects without breaking themselves.

Meditation and Martial Arts Magic

Can meditation offer special insights into Martial Arts?

Meditation and Martial Arts have gone hand in hand for Millennia. After all both originate in Asia, both have connections to religion and both offer unique insights into the human body...

...or do they?

When people think of meditation the most common image is that of the stereotypical monk, isolated halfway up a mountain and achieving some spiritual enlightenment that the rest of us can't hope to comprehend. (Just like that chap in the picture) Since many of us are not familiar with the intricacies of different Buddhist practices this then becomes associated with another group of monks, famed for both meditation and Martial Arts; The Shaolin.

Hence the assumption that Meditation is essential for top Martial Arts performance and that through some mix of Shaolin training, quiet contemplation and Buddhism we can all discover some hidden ability.

Most individuals assume meditation was conceived in Asia. While it has been widely practiced there since ancient times, it was also utilized by the natives of many other cultures for thousands of years.

Native Americans for example used meditation heavily in their spiritual quests while in ancient Latin, a similar word "meditari" – the origin of the term, referred to concentrated studies, which would have required much focus to master. In the modern world it is used as an exercise for the mind to attain greater balance and sometimes enlightenment.

As with any holistic practice there has been wide debate on the usefulness of meditation. Its efficacy is hard to prove since it is such a personal activity which occurs largely in one's psyche but has potential physiological effects. This is after all a mostly spiritual and not scientific practice. It can be associated with religious practices like Buddhism, or Taoism, but can also be practiced separate from any sort of faction.

Many people think that Meditation is a fairly complex process but in reality it can be straight forward, easy and effective for health, stress and wellness.

You can discover more in my book; 'How to Meditate in Just 2 Minutes'. My goal here is not to teach you how to master the skill; I'll leave that to the full length book, but to point out the truth behind of some of its supposed powers.

At the heart of meditation is one word: relaxation. This is found in a still body and calm mind. Many forms of mediation are done sitting or standing still in a quiet setting. However, there are also active varieties such as walking meditations. In nearly all cases the goal is to focus the mind by emptying out all the clutter.

Some forms require interesting body positioning, many resembling twisted pretzels, though in my experience the best work is done when the body is comfortable. Any discomfort will only distract the mind.

Then comes the confusing part. Some people meditate by emptying the mind of all consciousness, while others focus on a specific image, or even a question they seek to answer. In the end, what works for one may not work for another so everyone must find their own path.

Martial artists may use meditation to focus their intentions and prepare for a grading, a tournament or even self defense. If you have practised any Japanese styles you may be familiar with a simple position, sitting upon the knees in a pose called 'Seiza'. It can be essential to developing a sense of discipline, since this form becomes uncomfortable after only a few minutes.

The Levitation Legend

While the activity of meditation does focus the mind, allowing all the clutter to dissipate and making way for clearer thoughts, it will not provide magic answers. Through meditation you may tap into your own psyche, but it is yours alone. There is no ancient god, goddess, nor ancient master waiting at your beck and call to send answers through extrasensory perception (ESP). One would have to be fairly narcissistic to believe such a thing. My point is not to discredit religion here, but simply to point out that expecting divine inspiration from 3 minutes in the Lotus position is unrealistic.

Meditation is great however for attaining spiritual and emotional goals, improving health and general well-being. Still, it will in no way shape or form cause you to achieve special abilities over and above other Martial Artists or develop enhanced physical abilities like the famed levitation 'trick' as characterized by alleged 'transcendental meditation' or 'yogic flying.'

Many old paintings and drawings feature individuals in the Lotus pose, floating high above their cushion or mat but the creators of these images are widely known to be using the images as a metaphor; visually portraying the inner experience of a heightened sense of reality and perhaps that personal nirvana known as enlightenment.

It's not an impossible sensation to achieve either. In deactivating the typically overactive parts of the Brain we start to reduce the way we interpret information from the Parietal Lobe (Spatial centre) of the brain, giving a somewhat 'floating' feeling. It doesn't always happen, and I wouldn't get hung up on it since meditation has many great benefits anyway, but a little practice and you may find some interesting results.

That said, despite years of Meditation, I have yet to physically leave the ground. Nor has this phenomenon ever been witnessed or recorded despite many studies and searches to prove or disprove the phenomenon. This leaves two choices; either this levitation thing is so utterly rare that only a handful of people have ever done it, always alone and away from a camera, or it just does not happen.

Let's face it, any form of flying, outside of an aircraft, is just outside the realm of human abilities, martial artist or not.

Many people also choose to center on a mantra or saying during meditation to bring about focus or 'one-pointedness' as it is sometimes known. This is perfect if you wish to be laser-focused on a specific task, say, completing a Kata or winning your next bout but others argue that the nature of human learning is by filtering many sources of information and single-mindedness does not allow for this.

With this in mind the best approach may be simple 'mindfulness'; the practise of being in the present and not worrying about past or future events. This allows for both the capacity for learning but also a clear and relaxed mind, useful to all.

Perhaps then we should look at meditation not as a specific Martial Arts technique or even tied to Martial Arts historically but more as a practise for general health, whether you are in training or not. As with most things you will likely find one method of meditation more effective than others so experiment to find the method that resonates with you.

Sure, meditation can offer a quieter more focused mind, improved health and lower stress – essential for combat training but these benefits are hardly exclusive to Martial Arts students. In fact a couple of minutes of quiet meditation offers huge benefits whoever you are. Try it now!

Using Relaxation for Attack and Defence

How does relaxation give you power?

While meditation is often connected to Martial Arts, 'relaxation' in various forms is also attributed to giving individuals special abilities or unique skills within combat. But how could a relaxed body and mind offer any benefits in the hard and fast world of Martial Arts?

This myth is probably best filed under the label of "broad misconception". At some point along the line someone erroneously translated *relaxation* into *power*. Those with the ability to find a deep state of relaxation or a 'zen' like quality have oddly come to be admired as having great strength and martial insight – enough to make others wary of their reputation.

The biggest trouble with this whole idea rests in simple semantics.

Relaxation by definition is after all, the opposite of power. It is used to describe a state in which ones guard is down. Outside of Martial Arts one might visualize relaxation as sitting at home on the couch watching television with the remote nearby. For others it is lounging at the beach, or perhaps even practicing a bit of meditation, minus levitation. All of these scenarios have one thing is common: vulnerability. While relaxing, your guard is down.

When you enter a relaxed state, the muscles release tension and the mind lets go of any anxious thoughts. Though a simple concept, some people have difficulty with these tasks. A decent martial artist however will have skill in relaxation. At any place and any time they can empty their mind and let go of stressors, focusing in on the moment and discarding any distractions. This is known as Mindfulness, which can be a useful skill as we've already discovered. However, there is something else that might prove just as effective in a fight scenario.

I'm talking about fear.

Despite being a sensation most people actively avoid, fear is actually an incredibly natural and beneficial emotion that reminds us to remain alert and cautious of our surroundings. Those without fear or in an extreme relaxed state have a better chance of falling into danger. Fear (and in turn adrenaline) causes muscles to tense up and prepare for whatever form of defence is needed, it is a primal and essential instinct. Anger is another emotion of use; it evokes an urge to attack an outside target, hopefully for a suitable reason.

Without fear or anger to get our hearts pumping and minds jumping, relaxation would have no real purpose. We need a good balance between each extreme.

Hit Your Peak

Interestingly a number of studies have aimed to asses at what point our stress or arousal levels become detrimental to performance. I.e. when does relaxation become useless and at what point is it needed?

In a self-defense situation for example your heart rate will be much higher than normal, but does this mean you need to calm your mind or make use of the increased adrenaline?

A principle known as the 'Inverted U Hypothesis' has long been used as a tool for measuring performance vs. pulse. Sports coaches and psychologists discovered that at a certain point our increased heart rate helps our cognitive and large physical actions the most, after this things start to break down quickly.

Over 115 Beats Per Minute – Fine Motor Skills like texting on a phone or writing something becomes more difficult

115 – 145 BPM - Complex Motor Skills like throwing an object or aiming at something using larger muscle movements hit their peak.

Over 145 BPM – The previous Complex Motor Skills start to break down but Gross Motor Skills like running or tasks using the whole body remain at peak levels.

Over 175BPM – Everything starts to break down and physical and mental ability deteriorates across the board.

The Complex Simplicity of Drunken Fist

One of the reasons relaxation as a concept within Martial Arts has become so established is because of the traditional Chinese art of 'drunken' style Kung Fu, also called 'Zui Quan' or Drunken Fist. This unusual combat discipline requires the student to develop a relaxed and flowing style of movement akin to that of someone under the influence of alcohol. The misconception here however is that the individual is 'relaxed' in the traditional sense – after all it does look that way.

Many people love this style because it appears so different to traditional fighting arts and hence they think it may be perfect for someone who can knock back a few beers and stagger about taking on all comers.

However Zui Quan actually requires great muscle control and focus, not just a bunch of flailing limbs and stumbling around. The principle of the craft is misdirection and unpredictability of movement through techniques imitating a drunkard. These are tactics that arguably require greater skill than even a normal Martial Art, since the practitioner must look off-balance but in fact be in complete control.

Does the misconception then come from the difference between mental and physical relaxation?

One benefit of a relaxed mind is that when one is relaxed negative emotions are released. This can be immensely helpful when one needs a clear head to think practically rather than emotionally. Clearly this would be an advantage in a fight. Though rage can be a great source of power, it does not increase one's accuracy or proper use of technique. Cool-headedness provides more time to plan and execute your next move.

It is hard to teach Martial Arts students about the emotions that will erupt during a real-life altercation when your life may be in danger. However we can develop skills to learn how to control them as much as possible and maintain control of a situation.

The Danger of Hypervigilance

So what happens if the mind remains constantly tense?

Hypervigilance is a fairly common but rarely discussed condition closely associated with anxiety disorders and even Post Traumatic Stress Disorder. It manifests in different ways but essentially it is a heightened or 'hyper' state of awareness of one's surroundings or paranoia of potential threats.

It commonly occurs in individuals after traumatic events for obvious reasons but even 'normal' Martial Artists and Self Defense enthusiasts can find themselves affected to various degrees if they consistently and intensely focus on training for potential danger and risks around them. The irony of course is that this mental tension is ultimately counter-productive and can lead to long-term psychological issues.

The mind needs its relaxation to maintain healthy functions, just like the body cannot always be tense or it too will become damaged.

The 'trick' then is to relax the mind but, when needed, let the body stay strong, taunt, and ready for action. Not so tense that you become your own worst enemy but not languid and useless. Prepared, loose but focused. As usual, it's all about balance.

Which is the 'Original' Martial Art?

Did it all begin in Asia?

Time heals all wounds... but it also hides many truths.

The years have done a remarkable job in concealing the eclectic origins of Martial Arts. Based on the most popular forms such as Judo, Tae Kwon Do, Karate, and Jiu-jitsu it's easy to see the Asian influence. Hence it might be also be easy to fall into the trap of assuming, as many do, that Martial Arts were entirely conceived and developed in Asia.

In opening your mind to other possibilities, it may help to define what we are talking about here. The term "martial" can be traced to the Roman name, Mars, used to identify the god of war. 'Martial Arts' simply refers to systems of combat and defence. Each system is usually made up of a unique collection of kicks, locks, throws or punches.

Would it make sense for Asia to be the only culture in ancient times to need and develop these kinds of defence methods? A quick glance at the history of war versus the history of peace quickly eliminates that possibility. The bottom line is that Humankind loves a good fight and as such, cultures from Africa, Europe, and the Pacific would historically all need to practice Martial Arts too. Remember we are talking about the pure definition of Martial Arts here, not specific styles.

Even the famously civilised Ancient Greeks were fans of both boxing and wrestling. Though these sports might lack the philosophy and extensive framework one might expect from the Asian arts, they still fall into our definition of Martial Arts.

There are also the armed versions of Asian Martial Arts (those requiring some kind of rudimentary weapon). These include a plethora of techniques. Many people are fans of the sword and nun-chukkas, while others prefer weapons of traditional Kung Fu – often innocent farming implements adapted for combat. (Tonfa, Split Staff, Peg etc.) Each of these styles has one thing in common: they are all utilizing tools for warfare.

Similar weapons used through the ages include a huge array of sticks, arrows, and javelins. In modern times you might consider an AK-47, F-35 Jets and Javelin Missiles. Though perhaps not as respected as the Asian ways, each of these weapons can be practiced by its user to a level of skill which resembles art. (Surely piloting a multimillion dollar jet fighter at supersonic speeds is at least as respectable as mastering Aikido?)

So who's job then is it to decide what techniques classify as a martial art, and which are simply too primitive? Where is the fine line between war and the Art of war? Someone go ask Sun Tzu and find out.

A History of Violence

I want you to remember years ago when you were sitting in History class. Most of us studied at least a few groups of ancient warriors in school. Not the least of these was the Spartans and the Roman Army. These fighters no doubt had both heart and skill. They trained hard, for nearly their entire lifespan, regularly saw conflict, and often fought without any weapons at all. They must have had their own version of Martial Arts to establish such reputation. Like the Greeks, the Spartans also left evidence of a pastime akin to wrestling.

Though the Roman and Spartan styles of fighting may differ from that of the Japanese Samurai, they each proved to be very effective over lengthy periods of time. One might also add the Medieval Knights of Europe to that list as well. These Knights developed an extensive fighting system all of which was well documented in manuals of the time, some of which can still be read today. All of these systems relied on great skill and training to accomplish a simple goal; to overcome the enemy in times of conflict.

Why should only the Asian versions be allowed to claim the title, Martial Arts? Perhaps the answer to this great divide lies in the history of unarmed combat.

An honest assessment reveals the fact that in the grand scope of things, the recognized forms of Martial Arts (meaning those from East Asian countries) are relatively new. For example, the Korean art of Tae Kwon Do appeared in the middle of the Twentieth century. Though some Martial Arts claim an ancient heritage, this is not true for all of the Asian martial systems.

For some reason we have also developed the perception that modern societies lack the fighting finesse of more ancient cultures. European unarmed techniques are often falsely characterized as being weak and inferior to the skill of Asian fighting.

Movie producers have a lot to answer for, again. Part of the prejudice lies in the way fighting is portrayed in movies. More often than not the star Martial Arts fighter is cast as an individual of some Asian descent, while the villain – a nefarious Englishman - sits in a mansion giving orders. I know several excellent English Martial Artists and not one of them wears a monocle or has attempted to take over the world. Yet.

Perhaps part of the misconception is because the techniques instilled in the Medieval Knights seem to lack one major pillar of modern Martial Arts. The manuals we have evidence of leave out descriptions of effective striking, I.e. punching and kicking. It may be debated whether this was a flaw in the fighting system, or an intentional move due to the difficulty of landing an effective strike considering the bulk of armour being worn, but there is little documented proof of Armour plated roundhouse kicks during the crusades.

In those times, wrestling was, as mentioned, very popular and often recommended as a fighting style instead. It is, in fact, one of the few forms which have survived the changing of times. For a while boxing was also popular in Europe, but interest soon faded following the fall of the Roman Empire.

It seems that the real reason Asia is erroneously credited with being the sole origin of Martial Arts is that Europe and other regions failed to maintain their unarmed fighting styles. With the dawn of more deadly weapons, the more rudimentary arts of self-defence were discarded. After all, if the enemy is pelting your homestead with cannons it seems moot to learn a good throat strike.

As a result it is now difficult to describe the techniques of aged systems such as that of the Medieval Knights without drawing comparisons to similar manoeuvres belonging to Asian Martial Arts of the time. This does not mean that multi-cultural martial artists have never existed, nor does it diminish the validity of their accomplishments. It is just that they have faded so far into history, that everyone has forgotten the colourful and varied origins of Martial Arts and their true place in warfare.

A Timeline of Martial Arts

The following is a broad and rough guide to the origins of the best known Martial Arts. As always proof is a somewhat fuzzy concept and many areas of the world lack hard evidence of past occurrences. At time of writing this list outlines the generally accepted timeline of evidence surrounding the development of various forms of Martial combat.

As always each style has its own long and winding development so for more information search for your own style's detailed origins.

Where do real 'Martial Arts' begin? – You decide

- 3400 BC – Ancient Egyptians depict art showing battle between individual combatants

- 2879 BC Vietnamese drawings show early methods of weapon combat

- 2698 BC Huangdai, China's Yellow Emporer prior to becoming ruler wrote at length about medicine, astrology and the 'Martial Arts'

- 2000 BC – Minoan pictorials show techniques akin to wrestling

- 1122-255 BC, Chinese 'boxing' is recorded as developing during the Chou dynasty

- 770BC Mongolian tribes introduce a brutal form of combat to China (and in turn Korea and Japan also)

- 648 BC Pankration - a blend of Boxing and Wrestling is introduced into the Ancient Greek Olympic Games

- 481 BC – 221BC – Warring States Period in China. Commoners develop techniques for personal attack and defense.

- 23BC records indicate the first 'Sumo' matches took place at behest of the emperor of Japan

- 3rd C BC Indian Yoga Sutras describe meditation based on points of the body – later adapted to Martial Arts

- Mudra finger movements develop in India, a precursor to many specific hand techniques

- 446AD – Evidence suggests Shaolin Monks practised some form of 'Martial Arts' to protect their estates

- 5th/6th Century AD – Indian Buddhism spreads to China and influences Shaolin practitioners to develop 'Shaolin Kung Fu'

- 610AD Evidence shows Shaolin warrior-monks fend off bandits and further involvement in combat

- 1100s – The emergence of the Samurai and their use of multiple weapons

- Middle Ages – widespread practise of European styles of Wrestling, jousting and weapons combat develop in response to the on-going conflicts of the time

- 1400s and Renaissance era – Fencing and sword fighting becomes prevalent across Europe as an upper-class pursuit. Wrestling is widespread but seen as lower-class.

- 1400s to 1700s – Styles that would go on to become Okinawan Karate develop in the Ryukyuan islands based on Chinese influence

- Early 1500s – Bare Knuckle Boxing or 'prizefighting' becomes popular in England

- 1532 - JuJistu develops as a combination of various combat styles in Japan largely thanks to Takenouchi Hisamori,

- 1776 – Taekkyon, a precursor to Taekwondo develops in Korea - and is thought to originate from an earlier style called Subak

- Early 1800s – Savate emerges in France as a mix of Boxing and Folk fighting

- 1882 – Judo is created by Jigoro Kano in Japan

- 1922 Shotokan Karate is introduced to the Japanese mainland by Gichin Funakoshi

- 1914 - Mitsuyo Maeda brings JuJitsu from Japan to Brazil where Helio Gracie ultimately develops Brazilian Jujitsu

- 1950's 'Taekwondo' is established as a Korean Martial Art

- Early 1990's UFC brings together fighters of multiple styles in an effort to find the best

Bruce Lee; the Legend, the Myths…

How did he do 'that' punch?

Ah Bruce. The main man.

Despite having passed away in 1973 you are the perennial source of some of the most implausible and hilarious myths within the industry.

Incorporating many of the other elements included in this book the death of Lee seems to have done little to slow down his reputation. In fact the demise of the founder of Jeet Kun Do only seems to have posthumously enhanced his reputation. This could arguably be related to the similar condition discussed earlier; The more mysterious and unknown a Martial Art(ist) the more credence given to their ability.

This isn't to say Bruce Lee wasn't talented. In fact he was an incredible athlete and probably did more for Martial Arts popularity than any other figure in recent history, but the exaggerated details of his life has long created a fantastical image of the greatest combatant of all time.

Here are some of my favorite rumors, both plausible and ridiculous from around the Martial Arts campfire, regarding the late, great Mr. Lee:

- Bruce Lee could punch a phone book in two

- A kick from Lee was the equivalent of getting hit by a truck

- Lee's incredible physique was the result of a diet entirely comprised of eating Apples

- Lee died due to excess stomach acid. (Presumably from too many apples?)

- Lee could hold a 125llb barbell straight out horizontally for a long time

- His one-inch punch could knock a man 10ft across the room

- Bruce Lee was the best fighter the world has ever, and will ever see.

Dismissing the more ridiculous suggestions, the last claim on the list is the source of much debate in Martial Arts since there is no recorded evidence of Lee in a genuine fight scenario. There are stories one hears about how he and several of his peers used to get in rooftop fights with members of other Kung Fu styles. Also, his *Enter The Dragon* costar Bob Wall has told about a challenge one of the extras made to Bruce on the set. However, there is no footage of any of this. Very few contest his physical ability or dedication, but numerous attempts to televise live competitions featuring Lee were rebuffed during his lifetime. (An interesting response from the man that famously claimed he could not be bested by any Kung Fu practitioner.)

Chuck Norris (now a modern legend in his own right), once stated that Bruce was very talented for a 'non-fighter', a comment which, at the time, drew much criticism from Lee fans but in retrospect is seen by many as a compliment.

In fact it's not just Norris that indicated Bruce's ability was mostly for show. Kareem Abdul Jabbar is on record as saying that when he and Lee would spar off-camera his 7'2" frame made it almost impossible for the much smaller Lee to get close enough to have any effect. These comments could be easily dismissed as posturing by Lee's opponents but I challenge anyone to fight an opponent over a foot taller than themselves and not have difficulty.

(I vividly remember a fellow at my former TaeKwonDo club that must have been 6'9 and despite not being the most technically gifted opponent he simply stuck out a leg and it was automatically at my head height!).

Many now believe that Lee developed his immense physical abilities specifically to be strong and fast in a fixed set of scenarios, which would include public demonstrations and on-screen action. Not in real life combat or tournament settings.

This makes sense if we consider the direction his career was moving. Bruce was extremely focused on perfecting his films and demonstrations of his power/speed in the spotlight served to enhance his reputation. That's not to say he had no fighting ability – he clearly came from a traditional Martial Arts background in Wing Chun and ultimately developed Jeet Kun Do, which is practiced to this day – but much of his talent was developed for the screen...

The One-Inch Punch (and How you can do it)

...Especially demonstrations such as the famous one-inch punch.

First made famous in the 1964 Long Beach International Karate Championships, Lee demonstrated his ultra-close range technique on volunteer Bob Baker of California, apparently sending him reeling:

"When he punched me that last time, I had to stay home from work because the pain in my chest was unbearable."

But is the technique in this case supernatural or just clever application of physics?

In fact Lee's most famous strike was derived from his training in Wing Chun, a style which focuses on compact applications of power. Within the Wing Chun community the one-inch punch is far from unique and in fact can be found practiced in most clubs to some extent. It is simply a case of converting core body power into an explosive close-range strike, instead of drawing the arm back. In fact this principle of core strength guiding striking power is what drives most Martial Arts today.

But Bruce knocked his volunteer across the room with his one-inch punch, I hear you say.

At this point fact merges with fiction and reality gets lost in-between. Most accounts of the famous demonstration indicate that Baker, upon receiving the punch was thrown across the room onto the floor, however in reading the detail it becomes clear that a chair had in-fact been placed behind Baker "for safety". Naturally, staggering backwards into a chair causes one to fall over and intentional or not this is a likely cause of the more spectacular accounts of that day.

This is not to say the strike wasn't impressive. Lee performed this particular feat in front of a live audience – so no camera trickery could be accused of altering what happened. There is little doubt Lee had a powerful technique in the one-inch Punch but perhaps only akin to anyone who had perfected the similar technique in Wing Chun. After all, Lee never claimed to be the only one with this skill.

Ask yourself this; If someone gave you a close-range shove into a chair and put their weight behind it would you be able to stay upright? Now imagine it was delivered by a strong and dedicated Martial Artist.

It's all in the everything

However Bruce Lee also showcased the technique not just against people but by breaking boards from a mere inch away. In fact you can still find grainy video footage of one of these demonstrations.

This evidence has been closely examined and subjected to numerous scientific studies aimed at understanding just how such a close-range strike could be so effective. The results have been surprising.

Most people would assume it is arm strength or the use of upper body power that turns the one-Inch punch into a board-breaker, and this is partly true, but a biomechanical study carried out by Jessica Rose a researcher at Stanford University shows that in fact it is the perfect co-ordination of the *whole body* that makes the biggest difference in delivering the technique.

Rose claims that muscle strength is only a small part of the equation and in reality the explosive combination of the entire body is far more important:

"Lee has combined the power of some of the biggest muscles in his body into a tiny area of force."

"*Muscle fibers do not dictate co-ordination,*" … "*coordination and timing are essential factors behind movements like this one-inch punch.*"

So how can I do it?

Biomechanical studies of bodily co-ordination and its benefits for Martial Arts power have also been studied by the Imperial College London. A 2012 study by Neurologist Ed Roberts examined close range punching strength between experienced Martial Artists and similarly muscled (though not experienced) individuals with no training.

The amazing results showed again that those with experience punching in say, Karate, delivered far more power than the untrained individuals, despite similar muscle mass. It turns out that the force and co-ordination of a strike is directly affected by the micro structure of white matter in the brain within the supplementary motor cortex.

"The altered white matter allows for more abundant or complex cell connections in that brain region"

What this means is that by practicing co-ordination and delivering whole body techniques we actually build and re-enforce the parts of our brain needed for limb and muscle action; essentially a little like weightlifting for your brain.

Experts like Bruce Lee would have in fact have built up this white-matter and as such could deliver perfect timing and co-ordination, not just brute strength. If you'd like to do the same the solution is simple; practice whole body movements.

Just like building muscle, if we keep pushing our brain to perfect a technique like close range punching or explosive whole body movements it actually adapts and becomes stronger; in turn helping us convert the entire body into a tiny area of immense force.

The Lee Legacy

Sadly of course Lee's life was cut short during the final stages of editing his classic *Enter the Dragon*. His passing at the young age of 32, at the height of his exposure, led to much speculation regarding the circumstances of his death including theories of; Triad Contract Killers, Family Curses and the official ruling at the time of; "death by misadventure." (Presumably a conspiracy involving Pirates and lost treasure).

The reality is far less fantastical and more a tale of one overworked and incredibly unlucky individual. On July 20 1973 Lee spent the day meeting fellow cast and crew members regarding upcoming films. Complaining of a headache he was given an analgesic to help with the pain. Later, around 7.30pm, Lee went to take a short nap and never woke up. He was eventually rushed to hospital but pronounced dead on arrival. While numerous experts have opinions on the cause of death, the most accepted theory is that Cerebral Edema (Brain Swelling) likely triggered by an allergic reaction to the medication he had taken, was the cause.

Sad indeed, but the reality of overworked, overstressed movie stars meeting an untimely end because of a reaction to drugs, prescription or otherwise, are nothing supernatural. Just ask the family of Heath Ledger.

Bruce we salute you. You may not have been the Chinese superman some people thought, but you continue to inspire thousands of Martial Artists worldwide and your legacy lives on in some of the most entertaining films ever made. That alone is a super-power in many eyes.

Thank you (and a Free Book!)

The world of Martial Arts is one of fantastical claims, incredible stories and legendary deeds, but among these we find that the truth is often just as interesting.

While you may no longer enter the dojo expecting to learn how to kill a man with a single touch, you now hopefully have a better understanding of the fantastical world of Martial Arts and which direction to take in your path.

So thanks for reading this short book. I work hard to create useful and easy to follow guides for Martial Arts, Fitness, Self Defense and wellbeing.

Positive reviews make a world of difference to authors and other readers alike so please leave a review if you enjoyed reading.

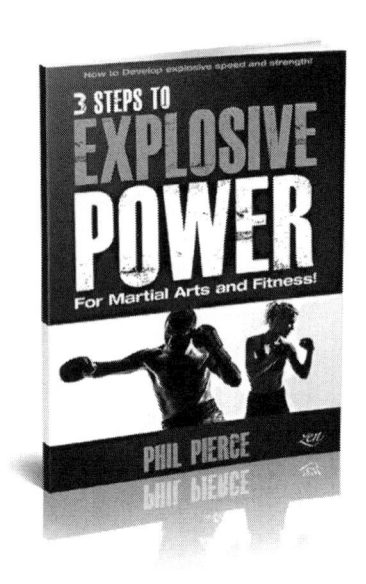

Finally, for your COMPLETELY FREE book, remember to check out my site at:

www.BlackBeltFit.com

Thanks again.

- Phil

Ready for More?

Check out some of the other Martial Arts, Fitness and Wellbeing titles from Phil Pierce:

How to Defend Yourself in 3 Seconds (or Less): The Self Defense Secrets You Need to Know!

The Original and No. 1 Self Defense Bestseller!

http://bit.ly/1D5E2SK

With most violent encounters the ability to defend yourself comes down to a matter of seconds where the right actions can be the difference between life and death.

Developed with input from Top Martial Artists and Self Defense experts this illustrated guide reveals the secrets of real Self Defense and exposes the truth behind street violence.

All designed to give you straight-forward, practical advice and keep you safe when it counts…

Fitness Hacks: 50 Shortcuts to Effortlessly Cheat Your Way to a Better Body Today!

The No.1 Fitness Bestseller!

http://bit.ly/1MsobzU

Discover 50 Simple Shortcuts for more motivation, losing fat, building muscle and a healthier, happier body today!

'Fitness Hacks' reveals the powerful secret tips and tricks YOU can easily use in your daily life to Lose Weight, Build Muscle or get fit fast! This expert guide, with insights from top instructors, fitness coaches and cutting-edge research, skips the BS and hard work and exposes the efficiency shortcuts and psychological 'hacks' you can use right now to improve your body today!

How to Meditate in Just 2 Minutes: Easy Meditation for Beginners and Experts Alike

http://bit.ly/1HUMDqx

Given, Meditation can be an incredibly powerful tool in improving both physical and mental health, focus and relaxation but most people think it takes a long time to see results. The truth is, it doesn't!

With this easy-to-use, bestselling book you can quickly learn how to achieve these incredible benefits in just 2 Minutes a day…

Copyright

This publication (and any by this Author) may not be copied or reproduced in any format, by any means - electronic or otherwise - without prior consent from the copyright owner or publisher.

All content Copyright © 2015.

All content herein is considered a guide only.
No liability is accepted for the practice of any techniques described within this book.